May 13, 1985

You will be immediately
  told that it is enough
  to have God.
But a good means to having
  God is to speak with
  His Friends.

S. Teresa

WITHIN THE CASTLE
with
ST. TERESA OF AVILA

WITHIN THE CASTLE

with

ST. TERESA OF AVILA

by
Sister Madeleine of St. Joseph, O.C.D.

Translated and Abridged
by
The Carmel of Pittsford

Franciscan Herald Press
1434 W. 51st Street
Chicago, Illinois 60609

159686

Library of Congress Cataloging in Publication Data

Madeleine of St. Joseph, Sister.
  Within the Castle with St. Teresa of Avila.

  Translation of: En esprit et en verité.
  1. Teresa, of Avila, Saint, 1515-1582. Moradas.
2. Spiritual life—Catholic authors. I. Title.
BX2179.T4M72513   248.4'820943   81-9795
ISBN 0-8199-0820-7   AACR2

Published with Ecclesiastical Permission

MADE IN THE UNITED STATE OF AMERICA

The Institute of Carmelite Studies has granted permission to reprint exerpts from the following material:

The Collected Works of St. Teresa of Avila, Volumes I and II by Kieran Kavanaugh and Otilio Rodriguez, Washington Province of Discalced Carmelites, Inc. ICS Publications Washington, D.C., 1976, 1980.

The Collected Works of St. John of the Cross translated by Kieran Kavanaugh and Otilio Rodriquez, Washington Province of Discalced Carmelites, Inc. Paperback edition published by ICS Publications Washington, D.C.: 1964.

Story of a Soul by John Clarke, O.C.D., Washington Province of Discalced Carmelites, Inc. ICS Publications Washington, D.C., 1975, 1976.

St. Therese of Lisieux: Her Last Conversations by John Clarke, O.C.D., Washington Province of Discalced Carmelites, Inc. Paperback edition published by ICS Publications Washington, D.C., 1977.

Preface

In 1578, one of her latter years, after a lifetime of faithfulness to the interior life, St. Teresa while writing to the rector of the Jesuit college in Avila, provided an interesting glimpse into her mode of prayer. She tells how she had been remaining up at night until one and two o'clock so as to get her business correspondence out of the way, being thereby enabled on the following day to give more time to that Presence she experienced within, so strikingly real and loving. This was her happiness in the midst of the many burdens that weighed on her because of the mission to which she was called by God. Both her mission and the experience of the divine presence were the fruit of years of persevering prayer. Indeed, at different places in her writings she explains that through an admirable gift of God she came in the end to an experience deep within herself of the presence of the three Persons of the Trinity. They were ever with her there, keeping her company, so that, though she had many duties in the service of her Lord, she was able, she tells, whenever free from them to give herself to this enjoyable company.

But prayer had not always come easily to her. Born, in 1515, in Spain at the beginning of its golden age, she entered the Carmelite monastery of the Incarnation in Avila at the age of twenty after much inner struggle over the matter of her vocation. Her decision, when she finally made it, was influenced, she recounts, more by servile fear than by love. The first eighteen years of her religious life she refers to as a conflict, a battle between friendship with the world and friendship with God. That assessment, incidentally, implies her understanding of prayer as friendship with God. One result of the many difficulties over this long period was her urgent advice to others never to seek a remedy to the hardships of prayer in the abandonment of prayer. In prayer itself there is never anything to fear, only something to desire. Even sinners, those who do not serve God, can find it a wonderful help. A life without prayer becomes, in fact, a life with greater trial.

In her conversations and writings, Teresa implored others to strive to have some time and place each day for allowing the Lord to be with them, even though they may find much difficulty in being with Him, as she did herself, knowing only disturbance arising from the many thoughts and worries that tend to rise during that practice. But the ending for one who perseveres, she insists, will be a happy one.

These struggles did not continue indefinitely. In 1554, when she was thirty-nine, a dramatic change took place in Teresa's interior life. Recollection in God's presence, formerly so troublesome, now became easy. Not only easy. Her experience of God's presence was accompanied by an inundation of spiritual delight and sweetness. She felt as though enveloped in glory. Her life was transformed; the life she was living now no longer seemed her own but God's.

Along with this new infusion of prayer, a prayer that she later spoke of as supernatural because of its passive quality and the inability of anyone's producing it at will, a new, complicated kind of trial began for her, one of the severest of her life. Her confessors and spiritual directors became suspicious and doubted the authenticity of the graces God was bestowing. At various times those interested in her case after considering and consulting about her experiences concluded that these were caused by the devil, who they believed, in conformity with the contemporary thought patterns, would often use women to deceive men. They pressed Teresa to resist her passive experiences of prayer and to try to distract herself. But the more she tried to resist, in obedience to her advisers, the more God favored her. He soon began to commune with her not merely through the contemplative prayer of quiet and union but also in the extraordinary mystical phenomena of locutions, visions, and revelations through which she came to deep understanding of many of His secrets and mysteries. It goes without saying that these new phenomena only increased the suspicions of her confessors. It was the saintly Franciscan friar, Peter of Alcantara, who finally managed to assure Teresa's directors that her experiences were the work of divine grace and that nothing was to be feared from her.

A part of Teresa's problem in submitting her spirit to the judgment of her directors was her inability to put into intelligible and acceptable words what she felt God was communicating and effecting within her. Her first fumbling efforts led to an account in writing of her spiritual life and was submitted to her directors. In this initial effort she had to reply partly on something she had read elsewhere. So she submitted her account along with a book about prayer in which she underlined pertinent passages. Only later did she learn and subsequently teach that it is one grace to receive mystical prayer, another to know which class the prayer belongs to, and a third to be able to explain it. The latter graces may not be given and were in fact granted to Teresa only after she had wrestled a long time with her own powerlessness in her attempts to express her experiences of God. In presenting clear analyses of the different kinds of contemplative prayer and in describing their psychological effects on the human faculties, Teresa indeed became one of the most skilled in the history of spiritual writing.

As time went on, then, this woman saint from sixteenth-century Castile realized that it was necessary to do more than simply render an account of her spiritual state and experiences. In subtle and not so subtle ways she engaged in teaching her spiritual directors with the hope that possibly some others would be spared what she herself had suffered because of a prevailing ignorance about the mystical life. The spiritual account known as *The Book of Her Life*, in its finished form, amounted to far more than a presentation of her "life and sins." It is a spiritual classic on prayer, rich in doctrine, both theoretical and practical, with her own experience of God's mercy and favor ever as the backdrop.

In addition to her painstaking care both to provide as clear an account as she could of her spiritual experiences to her confessors and to explain all that she came to perceive about spiritual growth and God's various gifts to those who respond generously to His love, Teresa sought to attract to the practice of prayer all those who perhaps would read the work. Through personal contact she was already urging others and teaching them about prayer as a means of entering into intimacy with God. Even some of her own directors in response to her entreaties and example made quick progress in these paths outlined by the very one they were guiding. In her writings, it is also possible to uncover the concern she had to free others from needless fears about the interior life, the kind she herself suffered much from largely because of the misunderstanding of many.

The Lord communed with Teresa so intimately, with such friendship and love, that she confesses to thinking few would believe her if she tried to be more specific about His special favors to her. Was this not what Christ Himself had invited His disciples to enjoy when calling them His friends? Understanding that God entered fully and unconditionally into human life in the man Jesus so that in experiencing Him His disciples and friends experience God personally present in their midst, Teresa insists that the way to divine intimacy is Jesus Christ. In the mystery of Jesus she found a human God and a divine human. The center of her attention was not the pre-existent Word but the incarnate Son. Since God Himself pro-vides us with the way to Himself, Teresa proclaims that Jesus Christ is the one through whom all blessings come, He is the path, the gate to God. How does she approach Him? By the way of friendship, the many forms that friendship takes. She relates easily to Him as to a brother, friend, companion (particularly in times of suffering and vicissitude), teacher, master, and spouse. He was finally her Lord, to whom she referred con-tinually as His Majesty.

Highly conscious of all that the divine Majesty was offering to humans in Jesus, Teresa grew increasingly distressed over the very few who cared about responding seriously to His invitations. Gradually her ideal took shape: small groups gathered around Christ their Friend, living lives of intimacy with Him in response to His call for love. Jesus was the teacher, companion, and spouse in the new Carmelite monasteries she founded. In her practical book of counsels on the life of prayer, *The Way of Perfection*, Teresa exhorts her nuns to humbly ask Jesus for His friendship and to live as though He were ever at their side.

As a central point, flowing from her own experience, she taught that the more a person grows in the spiritual life the more he or she will be accompanied by Christ and walk in His presence. This nearness of the Lord is more important and more significant than the many special and extraordinary graces she describes and of which it is the principle. The core of the final three dwelling places of her *Interior Castle* could be ex-pressed as the Christian fully present to Jesus present.

Animated as she was by the presence of an object-person (Jesus Christ, God, the Trinity), Teresa in her meticulous analysis of the psychological repercussions that prayer can occasion is in fact examining the effects that loving contact with the divine Guest may have. In its intimate reality as God's self-communication to the soul, the divine presence is experienced obscurely at the threshold of the spiritual life; then in Jesus, more or less, as the spiritual journey progresses; finally, as Trinitarian. And Christ's words of promise in John's Gospel are realized. Dynamic and operative, this divine presence is rightly envisaged by Teresa as friendship or personal communion.

In her *Interior Castle*, her best developed work, Teresa expounds the journey of prayer from its beginnings to the ultimate stage of a vivid union with God. Writing for her spiritual directors, confessors, and others who might benefit, she has especially in mind her Sisters, all her daughters, who in following her lead vowed to withdraw into solitude and live a life of prayer in small communities gathered round Jesus Christ. At the time of writing the *Interior Castle*, she had already founded twelve of her little monasteries. Since in their poverty and their solitude her nuns had little to comfort them from the world outside, Teresa asks them to look for all their happiness inside, in the Lord, and to find their delight in this spacious and beautiful castle each of them has within.

After her death in 1582, as the years went on, Teresa's writings spread, through translations, to many countries, and her doctrine attracted not just the select few who felt called to be her followers but large numbers of the faithful seeking to answer Christ's invitations by living deeply and generously. This universal appeal of Teresa's work recently received special recognition from the Church. In 1971, Paul VI proclaimed Teresa a doctor of the Church, the first woman to be so named. In doing this, he spoke for many when he called her "a teacher of marvelous profundity."

Teresa's little communities also spread through the world and have continued in her spirit to our time. Sister Madeleine de Saint Joseph, a Discalced Carmelite nun from one of these communities in France, offers us in this book fresh and profound insights into Teresa's teaching as developed mainly in the *Interior Castle*. Particularly successful in accentuating the substance of the Teresian teaching, which seems never to lose its power to inspire, her interpretation is both enlightening and appealing for our age. She has the gift as well to remain true to the demands and the depth of the message. We can be grateful to the Carmelite nuns in Pittsford, New York, for preparing this translation for English-speaking readers.

Kieran Kavanaugh, O.C.D.
Carmelite Monastery
Brookline, Massachusetts

Translator's Note

I used to wonder why any one wrote Author's or Translator's Notes. But having become a translator, now I know: it is not a dry list of names, but the answer to a need of the heart to express its gratitude to those behind the scene, without whom the book would never have come to light.

As the prime cause of this translation, first place goes to Fr. Albert Bourke, O.C.D. who made the incredible suggestion that I get it published, and then continued to encourage my labors to their very end. In the actual process of translating the unabridged work, Terre Haute Carmel played an indispensable part, going over the pages word by word, and doing endless typing, word by word also. Fr. Robert O'Riley, O.P. contributed a most valuable editing of the original pages, a contribution whose value carries over into the present abridged edition, except where the abridger may have cancelled out his work. For the final edition a friend, J. Gregory Doyle, deserves most grateful mention for having had his secretary type up the completed pages. My gratitude is also due to Fr. Kieran Kavanaugh, O.C.D. for presenting so helpful a background from St. Teresa's life and teaching.

Most of all I am grateful to Sr. Madeleine herself, who trusted me not only to translate, but even to abridge, her beautiful study.

May God reward each of the above by granting many graces of prayer to them as well as to those who will read these pages which owe their existence to the help so generously given!

CONTENTS

SOME PRACTICAL REFLECTIONS   **227**

I

By Way of Introduction

The *Interior Castle* is the masterpiece of St. Teresa's writings on prayer. In it she describes spiritual progress in seven stages which she names "mansions" or "dwelling places": "I thought of the soul as resembling a castle, built out of a single diamond . . . and containing many rooms, just as in heaven there are many mansions" (see Jn 14, 2; 1, 1, 4). "I have only mentioned seven mansions, yet each one contains many more" (Epilogue).[1]

It is evident that what she has in mind is the feudal castle with its successive enclosures, for she adds: "You must not think of a suite of rooms placed in succession . . . (rather) they are like a kernal of a palmito[2] from which several rinds must be removed before coming to the eatable part; the chief chamber is surrounded by a large number of others."[3] Teresa keeps to this centric and convergent arrangement which has an important meaning in her doctrine: the Lord resides in this central room of the castle and everything gravitates around him. The symbols are those of another day, but her teaching is perennially relevant.

Confronted, as we are, by the ever greater power of a material and technical world, we risk misunderstanding our own interior powers, because they are not of the same order and are seldom visible. By living his true life, a spiritual man reveals man to himself, helping him to savor his own mystery and to desire to live it.

In introducing us to the interior castle of our soul, St. Teresa puts us from the beginning in a "mystical" atmosphere, that is, in a climate in which every action tends toward fulfilling the interior life, which is the source of authenticity.

Souls today are hungering to achieve this authenticity—to discover their true nature in the very center of self; it is there that the true Christian life of the will is born, a life which we can designate as the "mystical life." If this life is essential, it must be possible for it to be inserted into ordinary living and to find its nourishment there in simple ways.

St. Teresa provides us with this necessary, practical knowledge by teaching us how to distinguish our own acts from the divine action and how both have to be joined together. An understanding of her entire teaching will permit us to see what characterizes and what differentiates each stage of this mystical life; how, for instance, the Fifth Mansions normally lead to the Sixth, and these to the succeeding ones, although passage from the Fourth to the Fifth is less certain. By making gradual progress, we shall come to understand the intimate relationship of our interior faculties with the Holy Spirit and to penetrate the practical mystery of the supernatural life.

There are two elements in the *Interior Castle* that should make us feel at home in it. The first is psychological: Throughout the book our human makeup, with its needs, its limits and its laws, is taken into account and the divine action is presented as answering these normal human needs and fulfilling them. The second element is evangelical: the doctrine of the Castle and the experiences related in it are all to be found in the Gospel: the promise of these graces, the means to obtain them, the reasons why we make much or little progress. St. Teresa says it all in her own language, but always refers us back to the source, to the teaching of the Master.

Not all of us can be eagles in the beginning; it is enough to be doves. Yet we do not get the wings of a dove by ourselves, we must beg for them: "O that I had wings like a dove" (Ps 55, 6). These will bring us, not an unshakeable assurance, but at least the secret of the true equilibrium that we gain by going beyond ourselves, so that we can add: "I would fly away and be at rest . . . (and) find shelter from the violent storm and the tempest."

We must make this our prayer, asking the Lord for both the right measure of reserve and of liberty that will save us from a twofold error: of not daring to look at high things or of considering them without humility.

NOTES

1. Note that the heavenly mansions are permanent habitations, while the Teresian mansions are normally stages.
2. Palmito: a plant of Andalusia.
3. I, 2:8. Henceforth, any unspecified references, such as this, will be to the *Interior Castle*.

THE FIRST TO THE FOURTH MANSIONS

The first three Mansions describe the laborious passage from the state of sin (First Mansions) to a virtuous and well-regulated life (Third Mansions). In the Fourth Mansions, the divine action begins to make itself more specially felt, inviting the soul to more interior fidelities.

II

To Know We Are Sinners

The First Mansion is the mansion of sin. We need to fathom the profound significance of this stage and how the question of sin concerns us all.

First of all, is this only a stage? Perhaps we picture the sequence of Mansions as a series of railroad stations and the soul's progress like the advance of a train going from one to the next.

As we have already seen, St. Teresa warns us that this is not true. According to her, the Mansions are enclosed within one another, forming one indivisible whole after the plan of a feudal castle. Or again, she uses a figure from the plant world, saying that the Mansions are like the fruit called the *palmito*, and resemble a series of membranes covering one another and enveloping the pulp and the pit.

The soul need not leave one Mansion in order to enter the following; rather, the soul needs to bury herself in the depths of each and to make progress in this way.

Therefore, even at the end of our spiritual journey on earth, we can never say regarding sin: no more of that for me. As a matter of fact, the Saint does not exclude a consideration of sin from any Mansion.

After the first two Mansions where sin is the great problem, comes the Third Mansions whose security is not too reassuring,[1] then the Fourth where sin lies in wait.[2] At the Fifth "all

hell leagues together."³ At the Sixth, the nearness of sin is
particularly poignant; even though past sins are the particular
consideration, they are seen to be a "mire" more present to the
soul than the graces with which it is laden.⁴

Look at the situation in the Seventh: "Do not imagine that
because these souls have such vehement desires and are so
determined not to commit a single imperfection for anything in
the world, they do not in fact commit many imperfections, and
even sins; not intentionally, it is true ... they cannot but be
afraid."⁵

The reality of sin must be seriously admitted and we must
not believe that even by living a pure and elevated life we can
escape it. We must acquire the sense of sin, learning how to
walk toward the light without stopping, but never leaving the
shadow of sin—which is good for us here below.

Yet, there are Christians who dream of a life in which, right
here, no sin can be seen.⁶ St. John says, to satisfy them, that "no
one who abides in Him sins" (1 Jn 3, 6–9); but certainly he is
speaking of perfect charity. Furthermore, St. John does not affirm that he who loves *always* remains on a level of love that
excludes sin. It would be stretching the meaning of this word if
we take the end, which is charity, for the means.

Some console themselves for both their large and small faults
by calling them accidental things,⁷ that do not exclude a good
intention. In reality, our faults are *signs* rather than accidental
things; signs of the fire of egoism always burning within us.
When a light cloud forms above a crater, we do not think it
happens by chance. We deduce that the volcano is not extinct.
In the same way, by all the little clouds that rise a hundred
times a day, there is revealed the human which lives in our
depths, the germ of every evil.

When we see a person of virtue and good will, we ask about
the nature of this sin which is hidden in the depths of his being.
What causes it?

Christian tradition, basing itself on the story of the fall of our first parents, states that the cause is pride.[8] We ought to go further and ask ourselves about the cause of pride; for to speak of pride without mentioning its source would affirm that it has significance in itself, lending credence to the tendency we have of confusing pride with natural self-respect, which is not without a kind of nobility.

Pride has a cause and it is a humiliating one. Scripture shows us this cause in one clear, but profound phrase: "The beginning of man's pride is to depart from the Lord; his heart has forsaken his Maker" (Eccl 10, 12). A similar teaching is found in Jeremiah: "My people have committed two evils: they have forsaken me, the fountain of living waters; and hewed out cisterns for themselves, broken cisterns that hold no water" (Jer 2, 13). The human "me," taken as the center of life, is the "broken cistern." Again God is refused, which leads to the reflex movement.

What is the meaning of this twofold evil? It means that the duty of objectivity is the primary one.

The first decision one must make is to acknowledge this duty. The dynamism of our being is created for this; it is the condition of our attaining balance. However, to do this requires a maximum of spiritual energy. We are creatures who came from nothing, and there is a peculiar tendency in us not to aim too high, not to fulfill ourselves if it takes too great an effort.

What happens when the drive toward the essential goal wavers? The creature turns back on himself. Instead of achieving true personality, a false personality is unleashed: pride. Pride then is only a second step. The powerlessness of raising the heart above itself precedes it and is the first failure.

God reproaches his people in the Old Testament with being "stiffnecked" (Ex 32, 9). Is this the ultimate cause of their revolt? The evil runs even deeper: "Their heart is far from the Lord." Just as germs seize upon a diseased organism, so also

this "tetanus" of the heart hardens it, depriving the heart of
health, in this case of its objective disposition.

"Bend the stubborn heart and will," we sing on Pentecost.
The next two verses suggest a way of doing it: "Melt the
frozen.... Guide the steps that go astray." What is lacking in
order to welcome divine guidance and flee sin is the enthusias-
tic command that must come from the center of one's being.

To sum up: the good of the soul, its primary activity, is to go
to God, forgetting self. Nevertheless, its natural disposition
causes the soul to make slow progress toward Him. And the
essence of its sin is its more-or-less conscious fault of omission.

This fault comes from deep within ourselves. It renders us
guilty, even when it is not expressed by any exterior offense.

In the most secret part of our natures, we surrender in a way
that words cannot describe or examples appreciate. This surrender precedes any perceptible fault, but it requires constant
contrition because it wounds the very heart of love. It would
be wrong to consider surrender as not positive enough to be
called sin. We are not speaking here of responsibility in the
juridical sense, but as it applies to the mystery of the will itself,
a power which is essentially active and which is endangered by
the slightest inertia.

We can see this in the original sin of our first mother. When
did this sin begin? When Eve picked and ate the forbidden
fruit? Before that. When she looked at the fruit and found it
desirable? Still before. She would not have looked at the fruit if
she had kept the strength of her will for the Lord. The eyes of
the servant which are fixed on the hands of her mistress see
nothing else (see Ps. 123, 2). They do not see what the mistress'
hands do not wish to give her; or, at least, they see it only from
a distance, without envy.

What is the secret? The Canticle teaches it in saying of the
Spouse: "His eyes are doves ... bathed in milk" (Song 5, 12).
Our look at every creature must be "bathed in milk"; plunging

itself into the purity of the divine will in order to see nothing except through it. Thus it will be a strong and noble gaze; a gaze of innocence, for innocence is a power; a fleeting gaze that is not compromised by the inferiority of its object. Sin exists necessarily where contemplative wholeness cannot be found. It begins as soon as this ceases. The first sin can be explained by a weakness whose beginning was very small. Consequently, the mystery of sin in us is a mystery of inactivity. Its source is deeper than the place where our "good intentions" reside; for this reason it can be ignored. But our will is also present at this depth, as much or more so than at the level of its "intention," this is the reason we have responsibility.

By causing consciousness of self to penetrate to this depth, the "mystical" life will make us perceive abandonment of God as a constant and threatening possibility. The humility of the saints is explained by this. They knew they were sinners without imagining it or affecting it. St. Paul used to say: "I do not do what I want, but I do, the very thing I hate" (Rom. 7, 15). And St. Teresa was not surprised to see her place in hell, the place she had merited!

We know she never merited hell. But all restraint in our relationship with God tends to cause a separation. To speak simply, there is fundamentally only one sin: to take a serious interest in something that is not God. All of us are more- or less-wayward on this point. And that suffices to ally us to what, for St. Teresa, represents hell: the darkness, the mire, the unclean animals.

"I do not do what I want to do." It would be frivolous to accept ourselves as sinners on the authority of these words. The knowledge that we are sinners does not require our resignation to sin. On the contrary, this consciousness puts the soul in a tragic situation. It causes the soul to live fully the drama of authentic life. We call it drama because sin and true love cannot coexist; there is no neutral zone where one can be in the shelter of the first while waiting for the second. God, says St. Paul, "has delivered us from the power of darkness and trans- ferred us to the kingdom of his beloved son" (Col. 1, 13). Access to the Kingdom is immediate, but the journey is a continuous one, failing which we are enslaved to sin.

We are *all* sinners. There is no distinction, St. Paul repeats: "All have sinned and fall short of the glory of God" (Rom 3, 23). Thus, there is no fundamental distinction even among Chris- tians, whatever their degree of perfection may be. Here below, sin, in its deepest sense, is the starting point always existing and often found turned into reality.

When the Apostle adds, all "fall short of the glory of God," he means that we shall never be delivered from sin until we live entirely in the realm of divine charity. Thus, we need not only a compassionate pardon, but also the glorious generosity of love itself. When we beg the mercy of the Lamb who takes away the sin of the world, at Mass, let us consider the way he goes about dispensing mercy: he comes to us in his whole self, in his whole sacrifice, and in his whole glorious Being; and we shall be healed in the measure in which we will put ourselves on his level.

This can happen only after long progress. That is why we must walk the whole road of the Mansions. It is also the reason why sin cannot be excluded from our lives here below. The soul that dreams of excluding the reality of sin has no real idea of innocence. Perhaps such a soul will become a pleasant glow; but she will not become a flame, because she is not conscious of anything in herself that has to be purified. She lacks the sense of depth needed for climbing very high.

Since it is so necessary to recognize that we are sinners, how do we acquire a consciousness of our sin while awaiting "mys- tical lights"? Again St. Paul teaches us: "Through the law comes knowledge of sin" (Rom 3, 20).

One of the profound effects of the restrictions that flow from duties of our state of life is "to increase the trespass" (Rom 5, 20). If these small infractions do not seem to merit the name sin, still they manifest sin, they render tangible that ever-menacing abandonment of God. Whether abandonment of God is caused by the sin of idolatry or atheism, or simply by the repugnance the creature feels at the prospect of forgetting self in order to desire God totally, the tendency is the same.

Hence, our little "failures" cry out what we are. And because of this, if we will it, they set us on the road to authentic life.

For St. Paul continues: "But where sin increased, grace abounded all the more." He says sin, that is, an offense, the manifestation of sin. There is no other advantage to having sin increase. But the consciousness of sin is the root of all good.

The fruit of the First Mansions is exactly that: that courage and sensitiveness to feel and to recognize in ourselves and in what comes from us the odor of sin: the odor of sin in our weaknesses, in our mistakes too, and even in our just acts. Effort has no meaning unless we see the obstacles.

This is what gives this stage a high spiritual value: in it the sense of sin becomes keen, an indispensable element for living profoundly. This sense of sin is not the work of those who sin. It is a consideration that belongs first of all to Christ, to Mary, and to the saints: only love can understand what the refusal to love is "You will know your sins in the measure in which you atone for them" (Blaise Pascal).[9]

To acquire this knowledge is to enter into Christian truth in the way it is expressed in the first Eucharistic Prayer: "Though we are sinners, we trust in your mercy and love"—two states which do not exclude each other.

St. Teresa wishes to bring us to the Seventh Mansions, but here we see why she wishes us to understand the First. Hence, we must not consider passing through this stage without stopping, but rather of living it in depth.

NOTES

1. "While prudence rules our actions all things obstruct us" (III, 2:11).
2. The soul advances "unless it turns from the right road and offends God; should it act thus, it would lose everything" (IV, 3:8).
3. "I have known persons ... who have reached this state of prayer, yet whom the devil reclaimed by his subtlety and wiles. All hell leagues together" in order to succeed (V, 4:4).
4. "The favors ... are so powerful that they seem to rush through the soul at times like a strong, swift river; its sins, however, remain like the mire in the river bed, and keep ever in the memory, making a heavy cross to bear" (VI, 7:2).
5. VII, 4:3.
6. St. Therese of the Child Jesus used to say, on the contrary: "O Lord, your child ... does not wish to rise from this table filled with bitterness at which poor sinners are eating, until the day set by you." The Story of a Soul, X, p. 212, translated by John Clarke, O.C.D., (see Note 4, p. 56 for complete citation) Washington, D.C.: ICS Publications, 1975 *The Story of a Soul*, x, p. 212.
7. "... accidental things." Because of this, we make false resolutions in our moral life: resolutions to keep a rigorous watch in order to avoid little exterior falls. This is an excellent exercise in self-discipline, but insufficient regarding sin, the interior reality which precedes every visible fault.
8. "You will be like Gods" (Gn 3, 5).
9. Blaise Pascal, *The Mystery of Jesus*.

III
The Problem of Beginning

We start with a consideration of sin itself. Not, let it be understood, just to discover positive grave faults in our lives nor merely to magnify our weaknesses; rather we must recognize that our resistance to taking an objective view of things is what keeps us away from a life of love. And this is the reason why charity cannot get a foothold in the very depths of our nature. Consequently, we even say "no," although in a hidden way, to the absolute demands of the First Commandment.

This truly is our sin. Indeed, almost all of our spontaneous actions bear witness to it, however difficult it may be to admit the fact. Because of our instinct for self-preservation, we have a horror of any object over which we cannot exercise at least some control. If this be true, what is our attitude before God, that Object who wishes to be the only Object? Usually, we admit in principle that we love him, but this affirmation is not really the truth, because our instinctive powers still look to the ego.

To progress in the spiritual life means precisely to bridge the separation that exists between love declared and love realized. The problem, then, is one of making a real beginning while being fully conscious of this separation; or, of the fact that our will does not truly desire God.

Here is where the difficulty arises, especially for "well intentioned" souls, and why we make so many false starts.

Happily there is room in the Christian life for new beginnings. After some false starts, perhaps we shall come to understand why we instinctively recoil and thus why our too superficial efforts remain fruitless. Having learned the reason, we shall go toward the Lord out of a true humility and finally take our "first steps" toward him.

Some impatient souls move too quickly; they are courageous, but they make precipitous resolutions: "I am not yet a saint! What can I do to become one right away?" Even though their courage may be strong, seldom overcome by temptation, nevertheless they are not facing reality. The reason is that sanctity is a "disposition of the heart."[1] It cannot be obtained by commanding oneself, for psychological development is also needed.

The following are the steps toward the proper interior disposition: Every virtuous act perfects the will; and, bringing the will to perfection, in return, allows one to make virtuous decisions, which decisions are more supernatural, more active, more sustained. There is a kind of reciprocity between the activity of the will and the power of the faculties which are its instrument. One sustains the other. The perfect act of the will, and the holy disposition which corresponds to it, become possible only as a result of long cooperation.

To daydream of being a "saint" all at once, either through the grace of a retreat or through good resolutions, leaves out the greatness of a perfect act of the will and of a holy disposition. As we have already noted concerning the virtue of being objective, the problem is to act with the whole of our being toward the fullness of a divine act.

When we say that such a movement is not spontaneous, we are not excusing a certain lazy kind of patience in ourselves; rather, we are remembering the true meaning of that effort which must be brought to bear upon the means, as well as the need we have of the particular help that God's grace provides.

This realistic idea of the meaning of progress is the basis of the doctrine of the Mansions. Many spiritual writers seem to be strangers to it. Exhorting us to run up the stairway of perfection, they present charity as something to be achieved on the first attempt. According to them, all that is needed is generosity in the effort. They consider special graces as a reward; whether such graces are given or not is of little importance!

This places the cart before the horse. Following St. Teresa, we cannot consider "fervor" to be the answer to everything. We cannot pretend that the Second Mansions permit us to say to the Lord, "My God I love you with all my heart!" except simply as a prayer. We still need to master our heart before we can give it, to possess it before raising it up.

Hence, we must proceed in a moderate fashion. We can make neither a very distinct nor a very daring beginning. Bear in mind that we do not have a sufficient psychological preparation, that we have to make the journey in sin, in darkness, weighed down by a resistance we can scarcely discern and cannot combat directly.

Two tasks present themselves: to escape as best we can from this interior tyranny and to combat the exterior obstacles that result from it.

The critical point is to know how to conduct the two operations simultaneously. The second, which seems more tangible and proves itself by results that can almost be seen, ordinarily holds our attention. What can be seen and measured satisfies us. This is why some fervent souls, and sometimes those who direct them, are drawn spontaneously to removing offensive things from their lives, thus acquiring beautiful and virtuous interior order. This is one result of pursuing the Third Mansions. Nevertheless, it is an incomplete result and we shall see that St. Teresa laments this fact.

Therefore, we must not deceive ourselves over virtues acquired in this way. They have only a relative value because the soul has not yet been completely enlightened, and in its depths the passions still slyly lead their own little life.

For example, in all good faith, we may confuse kindness with charity, or conformity with obedience. Our respect may be tinged with servility; we may equate "zeal" with rash judgments; simplicity turns into bluntness; love of justice to narrowness; etc.

Our environment and education may also produce "virtuous" habits which are less interior than we may think. Some unforeseen event or several exacting responsibilities may reveal great weaknesses in what seemed to be impeccable behavior.

Accidental aspects of virtue, such as customs and traditions, also occasion false attitudes. Some say that customs and traditions have an absolute value, others disdain them as trifles. The first lack a feeling for the essential; the others for the rhythm of life which makes one appreciate the value of the secondary notes of a harmony, the support of the accompaniment.

The love of self remains vividly alive. While we long for sanctity, we still protect ourselves from even the minor suspicions of others by some little preventive word which directs their judgment toward someone else.

Such a thing is important when the life of charity is in question, We will say: "I spoke without reflection!" This is exactly what is significant. Protected by self-righteous intentions, the kingdom of "self" is so well organized that its passive defenses function automatically.

The preceding is a rough outline of incomplete virtue. We need not be surprised or scandalized, for our reactions are unconscious. As long as the soul lives on the superficial level of "good will," it does not see the imperfect, automatic reactions which more or less govern it.

Operating on a spiritual life of this type is like weeding without pulling up the roots. Or again, these incomplete virtues are like cuttings cultivated in pots, which can scarcely produce anything but leaves and flowers.

What then is true virtue? It is a plant with long roots, sown in the earth by the Lord himself. The seed sleeps there for a long time. It germinates according to the favorability of the climate and whether the soil is fertile and well tilled. Its roots will go deep and it will bear fruit.

The principal thing is to dig into the soil, that is to say, into the depths of the soul. Otherwise one simply grows weary cultivating virtues that are like fragile plants. This concern for success is deceptive, impeding true progress—and it happens more frequently than we may think. Without doubt there would be more saints in the Church, if it were realized how artificial are virtues that are formed by direct effort.

How many people would have truly fulfilled their Christian or religious vocation, free from suffering more, if they had known how to make a strong beginning and how to avoid placing themselves on a siding after a few turns of the wheels.

Why is our interior life so neglected? Why is there so much of the superficial in our lives? There are many reasons. For some, natural limits intervene; for others, fidelity to the principles accepted in their youth has grown insensitive, and they have never known how to develop it as something deeply ingrained in them. For many, trusting in words keeps them at a distance from fulfilling themselves. The interior life must go beyond verbal expression by an understanding without words; this understanding depends on forgetfulness of self as its most important aspect.

There is also a certain fervor which thrives on ingenious ideas and warm sentiments but does not know how to find the pure, simple road of the "spirit." It drowns itself in its own effervescence.

The big reason at the root of it all is that interior growth and abnegation are connected things.

What follows cannot interest souls who are content with

their own good intentions and who are not anxious about the emptiness within. Deep interior awareness calls to an ever greater understanding of self. But the mere illusion of equilibrium calls to nothing, preventing one from finding the strength to seek for the Lord as he wishes to be sought in order to let himself be found.

We do not mean that these half-virtues and the often courageous attempts which produce them are not praiseworthy things. They are simply insufficient. They are not on the level of life "in spirit and in truth."

NOTE

1. St. Therese of Lisieux, Her Last Conversations trans. Fr. John Clarke O.C.D. Washington, D.C.: ICS Publications, 1977, p. 129.

IV
First Steps

Both interior formation and exterior formation must be pursued at the same time.

How? St. Teresa teaches us the way in her chapter on the Second Mansions, where it is clear she does not separate one formation from the other. It is ourselves who, through a subconscious formalism and a half-hearted generosity, are apt to cultivate everything superficially, even the virtues themselves.

In this chapter, we shall give the broad outlines of what will bring us to this practice in depth. Then we shall try to discover the meaning of it all.

The Saint warns us that this is a difficult stage.[1] If it is painful to combat exterior habits, it is still more difficult to resist those interior currents which represent the different forms of egotistical tendencies. When a visible good is pursued, the personal instinct finds something to satisfy itself in the very effort; but to attack this instinct directly is to unleash a lively rebellion. Furthermore, we are told that here the "demons" or, if you prefer, all that is base and human in us, "make a great confusion."[2]

It is necessary, then, to "hold fast" through reason and faith. Such is the second warning given to us.[3] To put it in another way; we must not count too much on aid from our milieu; rather, we must mobilize the living forces of our spirit in view of an always-personal engagement. When the question is one of confronting self in depth, education, example, the best of coun-

sels, all leave the Christian to his own experience and responsibility.

From the very beginning we must persuade ourselves that
the life of love is not in the air that we breathe. It does not work
itself out automatically. "One will be taken and one will be
left" (Mt 24, 41); the Lord directs these words to people who
live together in great intimacy.

What is the proper work of reason and of faith in the Second
Mansions? St. Teresa says it is "to make little of oneself"; "to
embrace the cross"; "to enter on the way without thinking of
consolations."[4] This is precisely the way of "objectivity,"
which begins as abnegation.[5]

Now let us try to understand, apart from all consideration of
feeling, why the first steps toward true life must necessarily be
made in this way. There is the problem of going to God, our
Object, but, as we have seen, for want of psychological preparation, we are nearly incapable of tending efficaciously to God in
a *positive* manner. Generally, we do not understand this and
hence lose much time.

There remains, then, the *negative* way. All the strength of the
Second and Third Mansions is in understanding this way and
in the art of following it. In order to comprehend its value, we
must grasp one truth: Our will has only two poles: God or self.
All our affection tends to the one or the other. Thus, to estrange
the heart from itself is to direct it to the divine pole; so abnegation is really an objective step.

Let us suppose there are two buckets suspended over a well
by two ends of a chain; to bring up the one which is at the
bottom, it is sufficient to lower the other. From this comes the
importance of little acts of renouncement, especially interior
ones. Our two Teresas not only recommend them insistently,
but both relate how they made their first steps thanks to these
little acts, which were so pure and profound with them.

It would be profitable, but much too lengthy, to garner from the writings of the Holy Mother the numerous mentions of these "straws" and the proofs of the esteem she had for them. In a few words, St. Terese of the Child Jesus makes clear the significance of humble fidelities. She says that we must "cast at Jesus the flowers of little sacrifices and capture him by caresses!"[6] We should realize the forceful significance of her instructions despite their rather affected form. Little sacrifices are "caresses" for the divine Object of our love by the very fact that they tend to separate us from any rival object. They *capture* this divine Object. The word is strong, but it expresses well the objective virtue of abnegation.

Here is something that will help us grasp what the work of the virtues must be. To cultivate such and such a virtue for itself, for the satisfaction of possessing it, is a good work, but not yet a "spiritual" work. That is what St. Teresa points out: this would be to build on sand,[7] making us take the wrong road from our first steps.[8]

In God's eyes, what is really virtue in the virtuous act is the withdrawing of ourselves from the tyranny of "self," in order to deliver ourselves into the sustaining hand of God. This submission excludes personal complacencies and the false mixture previously noted. Thus, a beautiful, but exterior, moral order is relegated to a secondary place.

Negation of self then becomes the principal element, the only thing which is truly worthwhile. In seeking for virtue, the primary aim is not letting it be biased by one's interior unreasonableness. This is the true beginning, which does not deceive and will lead us far.

These first steps are painful, while advancing is imperceptible, and the risk of falling back continual. Our Saint says this again and again.

Later, when the negation of self begins to bear fruit, when the Lord himself induces it by his graces, it will become delectable and will be perceived as a vital act. We will not fear then to "let the bucket descend," and to put ourselves in it. We will not be afraid to go down into a dark hole: does not love carry its own light within itself?

But this is not yet possible, for we are divided. The will toward renouncement confronts a "subconscious" which is still encumbered with self. And there are a thousand little spiritual barriers that constantly deter us and cause us to make imperceptible detours: unconscious sensitivity, an innate passion for being right, vexation because of obstacles or humiliations, well-preserved memories of wounds received, subtle reprisals, a smiling excuse—or a dramatic one—at every approach of blame, a mania for speaking of oneself, etc.

All these things we suppose to be involuntary, but they hold back the work of interior growing. Sometimes we are too near ourselves to be able to measure the obstacle, although we may feel, when God gives the grace, that we are marking time in one place.

How do we get out of this impasse? By truly strong actions We are not capable of them. By desires which are truly efficacious? We have to admit that we are not yet capable of them.

How about other ways? To try to efface oneself—at least to aspire to this effacement—or, less still to begin to perceive it as a normal part of our lives. It is still too much to attempt.

What is possible is simply to suffer in darkness, to suffer from not knowing what is to be done or to be willed. It is the pain of the little bird on the edge of the nest: its mother invites it into the air, but it does not know how to open its wings.

Let us note, however, that this pain is worth more than the tranquillity of the day before when it did not even look outside the nest. This is preparing for the next day's flight. The feeling of powerlessness is then a grace, a promise. Many, many souls, sometimes even after long years, are not conscious of having stopped, and live satisfied with their supposed acquisitions!

This anxiety, which St. Teresa notes with insistence as

characteristic of the true beginning,[9] is actually a mark of serious search, one which will go far and deep. For if we do not suffer from not knowing how to realize what we wish, it is that we do not truly wish it. We have passions; if they do not feel this misery, it is because they are spread abroad and satisfy themselves in other ways.

Wherefore, we must not try to rid outselves of such pain. Few Christians realize this because it is painful to concentrate the heart, and they prefer to serve God by more exterior works. Nevertheless, this way opens the road of the "spirit."

Besides, if it is real, it is dynamic. Like all sorrow, it desires to be assuaged and so it stirs up one's moral energies. Under this pressure, we return humbly, and much more ardently, to all the little acts of renouncement. We give ourselves to this less from principle than from need. It is very great progress. And spiritual sensitivity, refined and ennobled by this pain, begins to detect the "barriers."

All St. Teresa asks of us is to accept the uncertainty of this stage by assuming the uneasiness it causes, and in the shadow maintain the course of negative virtue.

It is the mentality of emigrants: we want to find a better land, but we fear to go there because we do not know the road and do not know too much about the place we are going. Nevertheless, we set out. Did not St. John of the Cross say: "To come to the knowledge you have not, you must go by a way in which you know not."[10]

The "objective" tendency is born in poverty, like the Infant Jesus in his manger. It is without light and without visible works. It is ignorant of its capabilities. It is a tendency which scarcely knows where it tends. It is, nonetheless, a precious germ—because it holds the soul, in however small a way, suspended above itself; that is, it puts it at the disposition of the Lord in order that whenever he wishes he can lead it farther.

We are often recommended to "seek God." This formula, like

so many others which seem very "spiritual," runs the risk of leaving us in uncertainty.

Meditating on the teaching of the Second Mansion, we learn to "seek God" by the only means at our disposal: "to embrace the cross"; "not to spare ourselves." To understand it otherwise would always be contradictory and deceptive. From this comes the extreme importance of the first steps.

St. Teresa warns us: "Perseverance is the first essential"[11]; the soul's "welfare consists in persevering."[12] So we must face a long duration. Pay great attention to this fact, remembering, moreover, that such and such a Mansion is never completely left behind here below. The obscure searching, the efforts on points that appear minimal, will remain a basic attitude until the end, for it will always be true that the kingdom of heaven suffers violence.

It is not necessary to exaggerate the thankless and negative aspect of this search. Life is beautiful, even with such lack of satisfaction, since, as the Saint says, the soul is sustained in it by the beginning of love.[13] And this seeking is itself already a sweetness: "How kind thou art to those who seek!"[14] It becomes even a beatitude if it goes so far as to be a hunger.[15]

This search does not liberate; but when the will, tied to its own infirmities, protests, by reason of its discomfort, against this weight of inertia and of sin, this seeking puts itself on the side of God—a first beginning of union, which is the reward of the seeking.

The search for God is a food. Our soul is so made to "seek the things that are above" (Col. 3, 1) that this occupation already suffices to nourish it; some saints have had experience of this.

The search is also a security. The impression of "finding," of "possessing," is perhaps an illusion here below. There is more spiritual substance in profound search than in a quasi-possession. And what is the true possession of God if not the final work of tending toward him and of going out from self?

Something even greater can be said about the pure attitude of search, for on his part the Lord also seeks: *seeks worshippers "in spirit and in truth"* (Jn 4, 23). Try to understand: this relationship of loving adoration and of total intimacy to which we aspire is a divine dream before being our dream—indeed, a paradoxical dream considering what we are. In creating us to be his, God has created a drama. The passion and death of his Son speak clearly enough of the reality of this drama in which his own dream of love is involved. If he deigns to condescend to take a risk, if he does everything to accomplish it at his own expense, if he seeks, is it too much that we should be willing to seek also?

The greatness of the "first steps," however weak they may be, is that they set us on the way to an encounter with this divine guest. To seek God . . . it is vague, even as a program. How good it would be to have a more precise and proximate goal.

We must see, and not hesitate to acknowledge, that this goal exists: the union of will in the Fifth Mansions. Everything in these first steps becomes full of meaning when, without false humility, we put them in their true perspective. The Lord will do much by himself to supply for their insufficiency, as we are going to see. But he will not be able to do anything valid except on the solid foundation assured by the Second Mansions.

NOTES

1. "Indeed, the soul passes through severe trials at this time" (II, 1:11).
2. "O Jesus! What turmoil the devils cause in the poor soul! How unhappy it feels! (II, 1:8).
3. "Reason shows it the delusion of overrating worldly

things, while faith teaches what alone can satisfy its cravings" (II, 1:8).

4. II, 1:13.
5. Cf. Chap. VII, p. 59 et seq.
6. *Last Conversations,* p. 257.
7. "Those who build on sand (by seeking consolations) will see their building fall" (II, 1:13).
8. "If we start with the false principle of wishing God to follow our will, and to lead us in the way we think best, upon what firm foundation can this spiritual edifice rest? (II, 1:15).
9. "What peace can we hope to find elsewhere, if we have none within us?" (II, 1:16).
10. *Ascent on Mount Carmel*?, I, 13:11. Collected works of St. John of the Cross, trans. by Kieran Kavanaugh O.C.D. and Otilio Rodriguez, O.C.D., Washington, D.C. ICS Publications, 1973.
11. II, 1:6.
12. II, 1:11.
13. "The will is inclined to love our Lord ... who is so amiable" (II, 1:9).
14. Hymn of the Holy Name of Jesus.
15. "Blest are they who hunger for holiness" (Mt 5, 6).

V

The Man Who Fears the Lord

St. Teresa has stirred us up to vigorous good resolutions in order to wrest our will from the hold of sin; now she treats in two chapters of an achievement she calls the Third Mansions.

Her pages are full of kindness and humor, and also of indirect allusions which must be read if we are to have an idea of the charm of her balance and humanness. Under the guise of kindly sketches and shrewd remarks, she invites us to mount higher.

Here we can only sum up the broad outlines of her advice to those whom we customarily call "good Christians." They have left behind the disorders of sin and the fantasies of passion; they lead a life that is regular, edifying, pious, given to good works and even to a certain amount of exterior penance (as the sixteenth-century's idea of virtuous behavior dictated). They are in "a sure way to salvation" and the Saint applies to them the beatitude of Psalm 112, 1, "Blessed is the man who fears the Lord"[1]

Such well-balanced virtue may seem sufficient. However, St. Teresa judges that, although it may be an achievement worthy of envy, it is also an unfinished work. "Worthy of envy" because it permits us to go further, even invites us to do so.[2] "Unfinished" because something more is necessary for God to be absolute master of a soul.

What then are we to do? "Enter into your interior," says the Saint, "go beyond your little acts of virtue."[3]

These words call for attention. They are not simply an appeal to persons "of prayer"; they make us reflect on the great problem of human and Christian conduct. "Go beyond your acts of virtue!" Virtue is not sufficient. Then what is the sign of moral worth? What is the meaning of self-government? It is the same problem which the scribe posed to the Lord in such blunt terms: "Which is the great commandment in the law?" (Mt 22, 36). We know the answer; it clarifies even natural ethics.

The tangible structures of Christian practice are not an end. Recall what was said earlier: there are two roads we can follow to true life; one leads to exterior perfection, the other to the intimate conversion of the will. The Third Mansions achieve the first aspect and ought to be a prelude to the second.

This is not just a necessity in principle. The task is a burning actuality. Even though sometimes we would like to believe that a simple kind of virtue is sufficient for "lay folk," the authentic teaching of the Church has never permitted this way of thinking.

The *Constitution on the Church* says: Jesus preaches to *all* that "holiness of life," of which "he himself stands as the Author and Finisher. . . . For he sent the Holy Spirit upon *all men* that he might inspire them from within to love God with their whole heart and their whole soul, with all their mind and all their strength. . . . Thus, it is evident to everyone that *all the faithful* of Christ of whatever rank or status are called to the fullness of the Christian life and to the perfection of charity."[4]

Thus all Christians are invited to live the love of God vigorously and in depth.[5]

How shall we learn to love? We can act childishly, getting out of breath in our efforts to stir up our heart, running after the idea of the feeling of love, as if trying to capture it on the run; but there is no point in such behavior. Love is more than an idea or a feeling; it is the whole being, drawn by its object and going out to meet it.

A departure and an encounter; beyond all definite structure there is that simple and radical course which could be called the decision of "no" and "yes": "no" for the departure: "yes" for the encounter. For there must be a departure not only from sin, but also from "self," which knows well how to coexist with a certain amount of virtue. We must say a "yes" that we have perhaps never yet said.

There are many ways of saying "yes." There is the "yes" of the soldier to his corporal, or of the student to his supervisor; these engage only the exterior personality. There is the "yes" of the child to his father, which tries to give something of himself. There is even a sacramental "yes" through which we assuredly give ourselves. But there are still great areas left undisposed of in the conscience, in the judgment and in the heart. None of these "yeses" corresponds completely to the full measure of "self." On closer examination, we shall see that this is also the case with those that we think we say to God.

Now God has a right to a total "yes," to an acquiescence that extends as far as ourselves. Our condition as Christians becomes distinct only from the moment this "yes" is pronounced. Perhaps many will never say it totally here below; yet, this is no reason for believing it is beyond our ability and our duty as baptized persons.

To love God, to say that "yes"—in this consists the whole true moral order; for it is an order of dependence, one which is expressed by the magnificent word "subordination."

The Christians of the Third Mansions are acquainted with the well ordered life; they must still learn the one wholly subordinated to God, which is the true Christian life. For them the way is open, the valleys are filled, the hills brought low, for their will is already tempered; it remains for them to follow interiorly.

Why is progress rare? What impedes it? Many simply lack the inspiration. But there is something worse than holding back out of humility: It is the self-sufficiency of those who persuade themselves that they do not have to give more than "edifying action." There is the great risk; a risk because it is a deviation from the Christian spirit. St. Teresa remarks on it vigorously and points out the consequences: the danger of weakening even the virtues we think we posses, for such an illusion does not stand up in unforeseen encounters; contradictions in behavior; surface zeal; disdain of neighbor; a claim (certainly not very evangelical) to being a useful servant of God and deserving of favors from on high.

This, in a word, is the mentality of upstarts, sterile because it is lacking in humility, the seed of all progress. Thus, the Third Mansions, if badly understood, can become a rut in which one gets bogged down in the mud of "self."

Are not the experience and the avowal of the nothingness of our works indispensable if we are to arrive at a profound "yes" entirely dependent on love? St. Thomas expresses it in poetry filled with wisdom:

My heart doth wholly yield, subjected to thy sway,
For contemplating thee, it wholly faints away.[6]

In all action there can be spiritual laziness. This subtle laziness—if we do not uncover it, if we do not escape from it—introduces the "flesh" with its cunning even into works that we believe are of the "spirit."

The work of love is much less to produce an action than to make an act. The act is interior; it is an effort of dependence. The true task of a Christian—whoever he may be—and the only authentic source of his good works, is the act which consists in "subordinating" himself to God.

"An act so vast and so simple," says Bossuet, and, we may add, so tenuous and so momentous, so naive and so profound, so spontaneous and so long in being discovered, that most Christians pass their life without having achieved it. This act is a mystery because it must be enacted in a region of ourselves which is impenetrable. It is also a mystery in the sense in which we speak of Christian "mysteries," that is, vital centers. In addition, the work which it demands cannot be a work done by ourselves. The Third Mansions, in order not to be a blind alley, call for the following Mansions in which the divine action performs efficaciously.

Besides, the search for the interior act is not an evasion and must never inspire disdain for the exterior virtues. In order to dispose souls for divine union St. Teresa herself puts this instruction first: "Let us practice all the good works that you know of. Let us do what we have been taught."[7]

These words call for the exercise of common virtue. They blind the contemplative life to every human formation, of whatever value. They integrate healthy morality and a good education into divine plans which we usually call privileged. They sum up the meaning of the Third Mansions, the indispensable preliminary for the following. The law must first of all be accomplished to the last iota, and fidelity to universal rules is the basis of every grace of election.

"Let us do all the good we know." This is only the beginning; yet, let us begin with it. To ignore or to neglect the delicate points of justice, for example, would be to render oneself unfit for the life of charity.

One virtue in particular corresponds to this demand for a justice that opens the great spiritual roads. It is the virtue of obedience, the supreme instruction for the spiritual turning point of the Third Mansions.

"What I think would be of the greatest profit to those who, by the goodness of the Lord, are in this state is that they should be more studious to render ready obedience. Even though they be not in a religious Order, it would be a great thing for them to have someone to whom they could go, as many people do, so that they might not be following their own will in anything, for it is in this way that we usually do ourselves harm."[8]

Today these lines run the risk of being little understood. One sees in obedience an abdication of personal dynamism—a paralyzing virtue. Is there not a certain nearsightedness in this misunderstanding? Personal dynamism is very weak when it is not fortified with strength from on high. Now, human work is associated with divine initiatives through obedience. If there is a negative side to this virtue, there is also a positive power which consists in seeking values above oneself, in capturing them at their source.

The incapacity of many in regard to the interior life is doubtless linked to this superficial conception of efficiency, which betrays a too lively need to acting by oneself. There is subject for reflections here, since the Conciliar decrees tend to reevaluate the life of essential charity, and since *love is a submission*. The Third Mansions achieve their full meaning, a decisive meaning for the progress of the Church, when the Christian begins to pass from the visible order to this invisible one of surrender to God, which is the key of life in the spirit.

St. Teresa clearly notes the two phases of this surrender: first of all, material obedience; the one which eradicates. It must be "prompt"—that is to say, undisputed mistress of the will. Then spiritual obedience delivers the Christian over to the "power of the Lord."

This double aspect of obedience represents the "fear of the Lord." "Happy the man who fears the Lord"—according to St. Teresa, this beatitude belongs to the present Mansions. It sums up the preliminary balance that is the work of justice—acquired and sought for.

In the strict sense of the Old Testament, "to fear the Lord" is to accomplish for his honor all that he commands and to fear his judgments. From the first (although it would seem without great enthusiasm), St. Teresa applies the beatitude in this sense to the Christians of the Third Mansions.

Filial fear goes much further, even to submission in spirit, since when it has done all that was in its power, it recognizes that it has done nothing and in a spirit of profound dependence awaits from the Lord the completion of its fidelity.

"To fear the Lord" is more than an attitude of religion, therefore; it is a psychological liberation. It means admitting that the government of self is not the whole of right conduct; that God, like a wise gardener, does not abandon to themselves the plants he has planted. He does not seek that paradoxical task which would consist in penetrating into the most hidden recesses of our being in order to carry out his commands in the full light of consciousness.

"To fear the Lord" is to render ourselves capable of his intimate direction. The "mystical" life is nothing else than this exercise. How, then, would it not be necessary in some degree for all?

Bearing in mind that it is not yet a movement of our will which can be perfectly oriented toward God and mindful of the infinite mystery which is its Object, we must conclude that the act cannot avoid mystery and that most often it has to be placed beyond our understanding.

Our true liberty consists not so much in our doing as in our receiving. Thus, the fear of the Lord is, in its ultimate sense, the feeling of profound reverence with which this liberty accepts the divine orientation. True fear, then, leads to true willing—the whole subject of these meditations—so that the Third Mansions, well-lived, prepare for the reality of the "mystical" act.

NOTES

1. III, 1:1.
2. "This is certainly [a state] to be desired, and there appears

no reason to forbid them entrance to the last Mansions" (III, 1:8).
3. III, 1:10.
4. *Lumen Gentium* n 40; *The Documents of Vatican* II, ed., Walter M. Abbott S.J.
5. In former times a kind of personal, closed mysticism was cultivated. "Interior souls" had to be reminded that the love of God must be accompanied by love of neighbor. Today, when concern for others is in vogue, such souls must be taught not to be satisfied with well-doing. Through his Church the Lord gives this good inclination its supernatural form.
6. Hymn "Adoro te."
7. V, 2:5.
8. III, 2:18.

VI

What It Is to be "Mystical"

St. Teresa traditionally wears the label "mystic." However, we may not ponder this word sufficiently to understand its true meaning, thus giving rise to certain misunderstandings.

There is the error of those who confound "mystical" graces with charisms, and perhaps, without being too conscious of it, dream of sensible signs of divine favor. There is the error of the "prudent." For them the mystical life is something special, accidental rather than essential to the kind of fidelity to which our aspirations should be restricted, something which a good Christian can very well do without.

Perhaps these misunderstandings simply come from a false notion of things "mystical." If this be true, let us try to grasp the meaning of the word itself, so that we can understand the real nature of the Teresian mansions.

We shall begin by considering fidelity that the "prudent" consider a sufficient ideal. We know that it is made up of multiple acts of the will: responding promptly to the call of duty; accepting corrections without protest; sacrificing time and work in order to serve neighbor; applying oneself to prayer when a thousand other thoughts need attention. This is what the virtuous activity of our will consists in.

We should be aware that this activity, even though it be virtuous, runs the risk of being incomplete. We can obey exactly, yet keep on coveting the work we have had to abandon;

refuse to excuse ourselves, but with regret in our heart; confuse with self-immolation some complacency in our heart, praiseworthy, but human; chase away distractions without achieving recollection. All of these acts may be highly meritorious, but they are incomplete.

What is lacking? Very simply, the necessity of the will exercising its authority not only over acts, but also over the source of affections.

Serious Christians understand this. Hence, they work at educating the heart by meditating on supernatural realities, by applying themselves to loving the Lord, by welcoming trials with love, by discarding human motivations, and by directing their attention and their interest toward the things of God. This is great progress.

But like all worthwhile progress, this progress tends toward a precise goal. It tends toward an act that is entirely interior, through which the will desires its Object, God, purely; not directly in order to possess him, but in order to participate in the act by which he desires himself. This is the act for which we were created: toward it we tend. Indeed, the psychology of the supernatural is unintelligible except in the light of this realization.

An act of this kind is mystical, being the essential reality of the mystical life. This is true for two reasons: First of all, because it realizes the mystery of our nature. Every man worthy of the name aspires, at least unconsciously, to live an interior life, but it often escapes him. Whence comes a mysterious aspiration which often causes anxiety. The "mystical" act satisfies this aspiration because it is situated at the root of our spiritual being. It curtails all our yearnings, because there is no deeper region within us that can give rise to anxiety and insecurity.

In this act, all the problems of our very nature find their solution: questions about personality (we shall come back to this), about destiny, about efficacy and the happiness of man and about man's worth.

This act also fulfills the call of grace: perfect supernatural equilibrium with the glory that it includes—*eternal rest . . . perpetual light*. Nevertheless, this act, which answers the mystery of our being, is itself something so mysterious and so secret that most Christians do not know it exists.

We live, as it were, on the surface of ourselves; and the first concern of St. Teresa in writing the *Castle* is to draw attention to these unknown depths.[1] This would already be enough to call her book "mystical," but we shall see how it is so in a very substantial way.

Let us repeat once more that the act of the will, when perfect, is mystical, because it calls forth, besides our own free choice, the mystery of a *special* divine action. That may astonish us. Are we such poorly made beings that we lack something essential for our task?

No, but we lack stability in relation to our end, which is chiefly supernatural. Our tendencies are somehow twisted and we especially feel a great weakness; hence, our activity, as well as our outlook, is nearly always superficial. We are not conscious enough of this to suffer from it, but we remain powerless to perform our essential act.

It is such a strong act! To say a perfect "*yes*" to God is to say "no" to all the sensible egoisms which make up our life, without our being clearly conscious of it. Thus, at times we are prevented from performing the work that belongs to us by nature by a kind of invisible wall, a mysterious resistance that is out of all proportion to the act itself.

In order to solve this mystery, we need the help of grace. For this reason, a perfect act of the will is called mystical; and, under the action of grace, even while the interior act is only potential, we are already living a "mystical" life.

Hence, the sweetness of the grace or even its more-or-less extraordinary character is not what give it a "mystical" value in the full sense. Furthermore, here the word "mystical" will never refer to anything other than the perfect operation of the will as it relates to our supernatural vocation.

Following the teaching of the *Interior Castle*, we shall try to see what this spiritual act is, how we can achieve it, and what its role is in the Church. This is the theme of our study, for it is the real subject of St. Teresa's book.

Even though she does not express it explicitly, St. Teresa advises us from the outset that what she proposes to teach is chiefly the disposition of the will. "Do not imagine that there is question here of unknown or unheard of things . . . no, all our good is in conformity to the will of God."[2]

We must have a clear understanding of the word "conformity" because it will be used often. We can weaken its meaning by seeing it only as a kind of passive submission to the commandments or permissions of the Lord. This sense of the word is only a secondary one in the thought of St. Teresa. Clearly she wants our conformity to be *in act* performed with enthusiasm right from the beginning; and this conformity in act is the same as the mystical act which we defined above.

Does not such a realization demand extraordinary and gratuitous help? One speaks of souls that are "privileged," "elect," "predestined." The facts seem to insinuate that this grace is rare, since many "worthy" persons do not achieve such fullness. However, we must take pains to avoid embracing unsupported views and not speak carelessly of divine predilections.

Certainly we cannot exclude the fact that the Lord may have preferences and be attracted particularly to one person more than another when it so pleases him. What we do exclude is the right of any Christian to say: "My abilities are too mediocre for me to be able to aspire to the mystical life in the fullness of its splendor." To say this would indicate a lack of intelligence that borders on blasphemy; for, to admit such a thought, would be to ignore the entral truth of Revelation and to fail to recall many texts of Scripture. One such text gives an admirable résumé of the doctrine of divine predilection: "Those whom he predestined, he also called; those whom he called he also justified; and those whom he justified he also glorified" (Rom 8, 30).[3] Whence it follows that every supernatural vocation supposes and guarantees a "predestination." And what vocation is more certain than the Christian vocation received at Baptism under the seal of the sacrament?

"Those whom he called, he also justified": this means justification in the perfect sense, since it ends in glory ("and he in turn glorified" them).

We can be certain, then, that on the part of God everything will be done to bring our souls to complete fulfullment. On our part, we have to "labor . . . to make sure (our) calling and election" (see Rom 8, 28; 2 Pt 1, 10). This is what is often missing. For, as has already been noted, there is a mysterious lack of understanding of the spiritual in us, an instinctive repugnance for carrying out the sometimes confusing deeds of self-purification that it demands.

If God asks for this pure activity of the will more than for anything else, if in spite of our repugnance, the proportionate means are available, the "mystical" life, as it has been described, becomes an urgent task.

The great gap in our lives is the false position we take in regard to this task. There are many "fervent" persons who apply themselves to their duty only in the measure in which they understand the extent of that duty. But some few do catch a glimpse of the almost inaccessible depth at which our true "duty" is situated. They are the souls who search for their essential act, who are ready to sacrifice everything to acquire this treasure, conscious that it pertains to their true honor to do so. Our every thought and all the virtues that are dear to us ought to be directed to this end—at any price. This is precisely what the *Interior Castle* teaches.

If we consider this teaching merely superficially, we shall fail to see its real import. We must let ourselves be drawn into the depths of the Teresian teaching in order to discover there the doctrine of true life.

We may think that this method and the results it obtains are of interest only to souls who take vows in the "contemplative" life. On the contrary, the question of the "mystical life" cannot be limited in this way, since it concerns the normal development of one of the most human faculties. Everyone must fulfill himself in the "mystical" act of "choosing God." Without the sovereign action of the Holy Spirit, no one would know how to accomplish this: that is, no one would know how to become himself. Surely, for many the possibility of such self-fulfillment will remain only an attraction; nevertheless, the road toward the goal and the goal itself are meant for all.

Here we have put our finger on the human reality of the Christian vocation. Outside this reality, the will has only an artificial life; what a strange error, to promote the cult of the will without knowing what true will is! The more-or-less predictable effects of human inclinations and their visible results are called "acts" and "deeds." We are unconscious of the fact that the will is an immense faculty which is only at home in God.

From the beginning of St. Teresa's work, in which questions concerning the will often arise, her doctrine is in no way voluntaristic. According to her, the work of the will is the major activity which sums up the response of man to God. But it is just a response, and is moved efficaciously only by the gift of God, who transfigures it.

Men are under the delusion that they become themselves by

an act of self-willing. In reality, those who truly realize themselves, the saints, stand apart from this self sufficiency.

St. Therese of Lixieux made a profound statement which perhaps can be best appreciated here: "The greatest thing that the Almighty has done in my soul is to have shown it its littleness and powerlessness."[4] She was able to say this at the end of her spiritual "journey" precisely because she had reached true "act."

The whole life of the will is mingled with a feeling of powerlessness by its contact with creative power itself. In this contact, which assures its autonomy, the soul feels that its act is received, although still willed and merited by itself; that its life is its own, not in complete independence, but only because it is given to it and because of all the soul has given up to experience this contact.

This leads to a rediscovery of a great truth: God is more in us than we are ourselves; to be us is to be his. This is the humility that is born of true life.

One question remains to be answered: What is the nature of this profound act which permits entrance into the divine activity? Very simply, it is the act of charity.

Then why call it a mysterious and inaccessible thing? Do we not all apply ourselves to loving God? Are we working in vain?

Surely not, but there are two ways of loving. One is in the intention, as well as, if it please God and the temperament is so inclined, in feeling. The other is in the very substance of the will. This latter is the spiritual way of loving. Practically speaking, the distance between the two is immense. And the long journey that the Interior Castle proposes has no other end than to force us to travel this distance.

Certainly, true charity is a mystery. Although we wish to love (and think we do), we do not even know what love is. Nevertheless, it is in use like a seed that takes root in the earth, and we must simply learn the way to achieve it.

NOTES

1. "... only vaguely to know we have souls.... Rarely do we think about what gifts our souls may possess, who dwells within them, or how extremely precious they are ..." (I, 1:3).
2. II, 1:9.
3. Predestination is the plan of God, wishing to save men; justification is the gift of grace which corresponds to this will.
4. *The Story of a Soul,* John Clarke, O.C.D. Washington, D.C.: ICS Publications, 1975 Chap. x, p. 210.

VII
The Brook of Gedeon

In human language, even in religious language, the word "love" can represent things of unequal value. Because of our hunger for happiness, we sometimes hide love behind a veil, thus denying this innate hunger as we often deny our other instincts.

If we wish "to live by love" according to the program of St. Therese of the Child Jesus, we must, first of all, know exactly what it is to love; we are speaking here of an intense love.

According to our Lord Jesus, to love truly is to give oneself. "Greater love has no man than this that a man lay down his life for his friend" (Jn 15, 13). Echoing these words, St. Teresa defines love as "a self-forgetfulness so complete that it really seems as though the soul no longer existed."[1] These formulas are to be taken literally, not in a poetic way.

In order to "understand everything" in the *Interior Castle*, we can base everything on one simple idea drawn from the two phrases just cited: objectivity. If it is not an appealing term, at least it is clear, and we need a clear idea to guide us if we are to walk with sure steps through the complexity of the Mansions.

Objectivity will be for candidates for the life of the spirit what the brook was for Gedeon's men: a means of providing the courage of the truly brave.

We know the Biblical story: Gedeon, who was raised up to deliver the people of God from the Madianites, had gathered

45

together a little army from which the Lord ordered a few to be
selected. The thirsty recruits were to be brought to the edge of a
stream of water: those who knelt to quench their thirst and took
their time at it were to be sent back; only those were to be kept
who would drink hastily, like animals who take a drink on the
run. Only those who were in more of a hurry to go into combat
than to satisfy their thirst would be fit for the great works of
God (see Jgs 7, 4–7).

In the same say, St. Teresa selects her own followers to take
part in the great combat of charity. Without doubt, she sees
everything in a loving and human manner, measured to the
normal capacity of the heart. Nevertheless, at the center of her
doctrine there is (as there must be) the heart that goes in haste
because it has been called from on high. This heart is filled
with a joyous hunger for the Kingdom of God; so much so that it
disregards all the happenings along the way. In a word, this is
the intransigence demanded by the Gospel: Whoever wishes to
follow the Lord, must "deny himself" (Mk 8, 34). (Mt. 16, 24).

The time has come to take a hard look at this aspect of her
doctrine, which distinguishes true love—to which all is
promised—from sentimental pretenses. Because now we must
be especially precise, the use of a seemingly dry formula must
be pardoned. Thus, the virtue of objectivity means that the will
performs its essential function, which is to establish a relationship to an *object*.

It should be noted that this relationship to an object, whatever the object may be, is a law of all being and is expressed
through their selfless activities. The sun gives its light, the
spring its waters, the flower its perfume, the bee its life to
defend the hive. And this giving is spontaneous, joyous, without any reservation. This instinctive generosity of things makes
up the beauty of the world. For us, our relationship to God as
our supreme Object is an essential one, and in the normal order
it prevails over every other tendency.

Just as the spring does not hold back its waters, without which it would no longer be a spring, nor the sun its rays, without which it would not be a sun; so also the life of every spirit consists purely and simply in yielding itself to its divine Object. There is something more basic here than what we usually call "love." It is, one might say, love stripped of every nonessential vibration. Does this mean that love is reduced to a skeletal state? No; rather love is brought to what is most vital and substantial in itself. The substance of love is to desire the good; and its vitality is to desire this good intensely. Objectivity is this dynamism wholly turned toward God; that is, an orientation toward God in the soul's every motivation as opposed to a subjective return on self. It is in this sense that the term, objectivity, is used throughout this book.

But to desire Him Who Is, to wish well to the Being who is necessary and perfect—does this have any practical value? Certainly God in himself has no need of being desired by us. Yet, the Gospel says that he "seeks those who will worship him in spirit and truth" (Jn 4, 23); he seeks—something is lacking to him that he looks for, that he waits for.

He seeks because he is love, and love yearns to give itself. Now, "to desire God," to adore him in spirit, is fundamentally to let oneself be drawn into his act.[2] This is not a useless gesture; rather, it is a response to God's own desire. This is the reality of "objectivity." Our Lord lived by it in his humanity. "My food is to do the will of him who sent me" (Jn 4,34). In a very real sense, to do the will of God is to will and to act in the divine act. Christ lived in this and he died of this; the work of Redemption is only a result. When he went to his passion and death, the Lord did not say, "Let us go to save the world!" He said "So that the world may know that I love the Father . . . let us go hence" (Jn 14, 31).

It must be understood our objective orientation toward God

has a twofold meaning. It is a positive activity as we have just
seen: a pouring out of one's being toward God. There is also a
necessary, negative aspect which is expressed in the "Deny
yourself" of the Gospel. We cannot desire God with the whole
of our will without renouncing the desire we have for ourselves
as ourselves. This extends to everything that concerns "self,"
and is as indispensable to the objective act as stone and cement
are for building a wall. Complete renouncement is somehow
the human matter of this act whose form, as we have seen, is
divine.

But this is what causes fear within us. The idea of negation of
"self" is opposed to current ideas on the rights of the person.
We are innately weak in this regard; our fallen nature makes us
turn back on ourselves, like the woman of the Gospel who was
bent double (see Lk 13, 11–13). Just as sick eyes feel better in
the darkness and crippled people prefer their couch to great
adventures, so also we have an instinctive terror of losing anything of ourselves.

Nevertheless, self-denial is necessary for all. Not only is it the
condition required for "following Christ," but it is the common
law: "You shall love the Lord your God with *all* your heart, and
with *all* your soul, and with *all* your mind and with *all* your
strength" (Mt 22, 37). Here is the dynamism of the divine Object
demands our very being. What is left to love ourselves with?

St. Teresa reminds us in the First Chapter of the *Interior
Castle* that "our soul is inconceivably great and beautiful."
This magnificent function of the will is one aspect of its grandeur, as well as the source of its increase in grandeur.[3] God
exalts those who belong to him. He does it by the very act in
which they let go of self and deny themselves for him. This
exaltation is not just a reward God chooses for them; rather, it is
a psychological effect of the act of self-denial.

What is discovered here is true personality. "Seek yourself in
me," the Lord said to St. Teresa.[4] The soul finds itself and takes

possession of itself by losing itself to go to God: "He who loses his life . . . will save it" (Mt 10, 39).

Does not every soul measure itself by the dimensions of its Object? "He who loves God is God, " says St. Augustine. And what a salvation it is! The saved ones become like the Savior; and the "saving" itself far surpasses our idea of it.

Salvation, then, is the creature achieving its pure state and its true measure by perfect adherence to God. Does not God himself give his measure and express his divinity in the Holy Trinity, the mystery of the divine objectivity?

It is because the Father is wholly in his own Object (Himself), that there is a Word, and that the divine substance has a "form"; and it is in the Holy Spirit that God realizes his "weight," the weight of love.

All men dream of self-fulfillment, but many do not use the true means, and thus risk dying unfulfilled. They may be honest, good, well-intentioned, etc., in the ordinary sense of the word, but they may never learn how to separate the pure idea of their being from the jumble of their tendencies.

Even on the natural level, "to find oneself" is to give of oneself. To tend toward "the good in oneself"—the proper function of the will—means breaking away from the apparent good of "self."

Unfortunately, the refusal to "lose oneself" can make our lives barren. We want them to be interior, but this incurable desire to hold back keeps them on the surface of "self." Hence, even if we are disposed for contemplation, we can go around in circles indefinitely, always skirting the fringes of contemplation, almost directly opposite the act, comprehending only its accidental aspects, conceiving it in a childish way.

With some, this automatic reaction can become as strong as it is unconscious. To what degree is this unconsciousness excusable? God knows. Interior changes may be so subtle that we do not know how to judge them. We use stratagems that are instincts of our nature which keep us from seeing the truth within us. Our enthusiasms sometimes paralyze our involvement in acts that are necessary. Because of these things, we set up hollow formulas, useless sentiments, superficial projects.

As a contrast to these evasions, consider the experience of St. Therese of the Child Jesus and the grace she received one Christmas. From the age of three, she had not consciously refused God anything. But, she was still under the influence of automatic reaction. She had not passed through the narrow gate.

At fourteen, she was permitted to cross the threshold beyond which love looks only at God; this is the grace of maturity. The sign of this new maturity for Therese was to no longer give in to childish sensitivities. Without shedding any tears, she stops placing her shoes before the fireplace. To appreciate this conversion, we must understand what this objective threshold in the soul is. We cannot comprehend it if we see in the victory of Therese only an act of virtue that she should have been able to make sooner. Because she had sought hard for it, she understood the prize that she had found: "Charity entered into my soul and the need to forget myself and to please others; since then, I've been happy . . . (I began) to run as a giant."[5]

For Therese, entrance into the objective life meant entrance through the narrow gate, with all that this phrase brings to mind concerning merit, power and goodness. It is through this same gate that we have to pass.

It would take too long to point out all the passages of the *Interior Castle* which refer to this. We shall content ourselves with a quick glance at St. Teresa's concept of the soul. It is like a diamond, she says, a crystal perfectly clear.[6]

This perfect clarity she speaks of is produced by simplicity of will, forgetfulness of self. It is like a spring whose water renews itself constantly because it never ceases flowing, like the heart of a child who does not know how to will two things at the same time.

To succeed in not mixing concern for self with the divine will is evangelical poverty. He who comes to the Kingdom with this pure kind of improvidence will enter there.

The Saint says that this will be so even in this world, and that it also supplies entrance to the Kingdom of Heaven. At death what happens spiritually? All the ties of the soul are broken. The only thing that sustains it are the bonds which bind it to God; that is, the objective power that it has been able to acquire is its only resource.

Death comes to the elect precisely to rid them of anything that detracts from this pure quality of being. Upon this purified foundation a new creature is built. St. John of the Cross expresses this concretely when he says, "You will be judged by love."[7]

In order to achieve this, we must not think it simply a matter of taking and keeping a resolution. The task is more delicate. The entire road outlined by the Mansions must be traveled, for it leads straight to this goal.

The Holy Virgin achieved complete consecration in the instant of her Immaculate Conception. Her soul is preeminently the "perfectly clear crystal," and her song, the Magnificat, the canticle of holiness because of its objective clarity. It pleased God to reveal to Bernadette how completely Our Lady responded to Him. Let us listen to her words, so that we may understand where she desires to lead us also.

Mary said: "I am the Immaculate Conception." This may seem equivalent to saying: "I am the Immaculate Virgin." But the Queen of Heaven does not speak imprecisely. The terms of the quotation she makes must be understood in their strict sense. "I am." But how can she equate herself with the divine act which made her immaculate?

A little reflection will show us. First of all, she collaborated in this act.[8] The more perfect the gift of God is, the more fitting it is that it be received freely. If it had not been given to Mary to accept actively a privilege that is also an activity, she would not have received it fully.[9] A simply negative purity would be too interior a sign of the radiant victory of the Immaculate Conception.

Purity in act is objectivity. Our Lady's privilege is an objective awakening, the most advanced, the most total, the most definitive possible.

We also know that the act of the Blessed Virgin becomes in her, in some mysterious way, "being." According to the rule and perfection of the spirit, it must be so. In God, "being" and "acting" are infinitely one. In her who is so near to him, there must be a reflection of this simplicity: The initial act realizes and determines the "being." She can identify herself with this act and affirm: "I am the Immaculate Conception."

The light she gives is meant to attract her children. No matter what distance separates us from her, we can and must imitate her who reveals herself in order to attract us to her. We must at least desire to develop to that stage in which a Christian is able to say: "I am movement toward the Lord!"

Therefore, St. Teresa rightly urges us, as she did her first daughters, "to be such . . . etc."[10] The transformation of which the mystics speak denotes the heart of the Christian completely immersed in his authentic act and revitalized by this act. This is the meaning of the Blessed Virgin's "I am," as well as the program St. Therese outlines for herself: "In the heart of the Church, my Mother, I shall be love."[11]

In order "to be love" like the Saint of Lisieux, we must "live of love" as she did; that is, we must train the soul in its act in order to stabilize it there. We must see the reality of this act. It consists in turning ourselves entirely toward God, in desiring him until we no longer desire our selves directly. No longer may we savor the gift of self or become intoxicated with our own generosity—both are ways of living for self. Rather, we must get away from self, closing the door behind self.

What still remains to be done? The deed of giving. This is

what constitutes the fullness of "being" in this life and, above all, like God, in eternal life.

The Prophets who speak to us: those who walk straight forward without turning as they go (see Ez 1, 9, 12); the ancients who "cast their crowns before the throne" (Apoc. 4, 10)—their glory and their joy in paradise consists in this very act.

This austere form of love is truly the kind for which our heart is made and which our heart must possess.

Much is said in the *Interior Castle* about "spiritual favors"; these are the progressive invasions of true love. From the beginning the author carefully distinguishes the ordinary consolations of the senses from what she calls "spiritual consolations" (or "spiritual delights"). The latter are the profound delights of the spirit in which desire for self is forgotten.

These are some initial ideas concerning the love which we all desire: to understand what it is, while admitting that our heart is not yet on this level, but still begging for this love and desiring it. In short, we must realize, however imperfectly, that it is a reward beyond our reach and is surrendered to us only by sustained effort. This effort itself is finally surpassed by a joy that is one with the purity of love.

In other words, when love has become a substantial reality in the soul, love is itself rewarded beyond all measure. It closes the circle of its own desire just as in God it accomplishes the mystery of Trinitarian life.

NOTES

1. VII, 3:2.
2. It is also to let oneself be moved by him: the practical aspect of love, which involves the whole being. We are here considering chiefly the *interior* sense of objectivity.

3. It is also the foundation of Christian optimism. Through it are understood the exuberances of divine generosity, the immense perspectives of our predestination and the measure of the hope to which we are *obliged*.
4. *Poems*, IX.
5. *The Story of a Soul*, v, pp 99, 97.
6. I, 1:2.
7. Maxim 56.
8. Secondarily, of course.
9. This does not mean that she put off the moment in which this active response was given, nor can we maintain that she was explicitly conscious of the privilege when it took place.
10. *Way of Perfection*, III, 5, in *Collected Works of St. Teresa of Avila*, Vol II trans. by Kieran Kavanaugh O.C.D. and Otilio Rodriguez, O.C.D., Washington, D.C., ICS Publications: 1980.
11. *The Story of a Soul*, Chap. IX, p. 194.

VIII
The Yeast in the Dough

To make good bread, we need good flour. The Church tells us this in her own way. It follows that not all are equally fit for true progress and true life. Some dispositions, consciously or not, are opposed to progress and life in the following ways:

—*the lack of desire;* we can go along piously in our own way, content with an ideal which does not lead us into a too unfamiliar territory;

—*a desire in words,* imaginary or sentimental, which leaves intact solicitude for our well-being, liberty, esteem, personal successes;

—*a desire in theory,* vain because it does not open up the way. We await the life of love as something that is owed us. We think we have arrived at it because we have entered a form of life which seems to include it. We have not grasped the importance of the "seeking" with its requirement of humility.

—*a false desire:* that which accompanies an appetite or childish esteem for what are called "mystical sweetnesses." This tendency is the opposite of an objective movement; besides, in accepting it, we turn our backs on what we thought we wanted.

Persons with such mentalities think themselves sincere, but they lack the foundation of interior abnegation. From this arises a lack of openness for which nothing can supply, for it is the activity of the soul withdrawing from self which puts it on the true road and opens its intelligence to the true idea of progress.

This is certainly why St. Teresa considers it so important for us to understand the preceding Mansions well: they are necessary preludes.

Nevertheless, the "search" leaves the heart in an impasse. How can the work be continued? How can we get good bread from this good flour? The dough is kneaded by virtue. But kneading is not enough in order to get good bread; there must be leaven.

Applying all this to spiritual things, the Gospel says: "The kingdom of heaven is like leaven which a woman took and hid in three measures of flour, till it was all leavened" (Mt 13, 33).

Is not the mystery of the yeast that of a special divine action adding itself to the work of virtue? As a matter of fact, the woman takes the yeast, she does not make it. It is something which is given. We are now in the presence of the second factor of progress. Throughout the whole of the Mansions this action will be shown us, accentuated more and more. Since its significance and its aim are not always understood, it may be well to consider these points in advance.

We must realize that the goal of the spiritual life is the surrender of the entire soul to the Lord. By ourselves, with the help of ordinary grace, we shall never arrive at this complete surrender, because we do not have possession of our entire being. Indeed, we should refrain from thinking that we have. We are like children who are titular proprietors of a beautiful palace, but to whom no one gives all the keys. It is the Holy Spirit who has the key to all our powers because he is their source. "Come, Holy Spirit, and fill with grace from on high the hearts which you have made."

"To fill with grace from on high" is, on the part of the Holy Spirit, something more than to distribute a just and abundant measure. Could there be question of two weights and two measures? Yes. St. Teresa suggests it when she distinguishes "general assistance" from "particular assistance."[1]

The Church lets us understand from her official prayer that a certain excess can be asked for with assurance; this will act in the heart as the yeast in the dough. Just as yeast has a chemical action on the interior of the dough, so also this new assistance of grace does not stop at simply sustaining our virtue, but works at a depth where virtuous application can do nothing. It reaches the vital centers and penetrates into the darkness of ourselves; it touches our life in its hidden springs.

This is that superabundance of grace which can manifest itself in what St. Teresa calls "favors." The word "favors," which brings to mind the ineffable goodness of Him who gives, must not be understood as meaning that His gifts are a simple caress or an overgenerous reward, like some unnecessary luxury which rich parents buy for their children.

If "favors" were not primarily a means of spiritual conquest, the "favored" soul would have reason to complain of its benefactor. Time is precious during our life on earth. To savor a sweetness which is merely sweetness would be to lose something. Each moment is good in the measure in which it makes the Christian advance in the direction of his essential "act." Would he want the Lord to be responsible for a hesitation in this advance? That could never be. God, who is always laboring (see Jn 5, 17), wishes that we, like his Son, should be constantly at work.

We have already pointed out and can never repeat too often that the substance of life in the spirit in this world is the search; the movement toward God and that greatness of soul consists in the quality of this movement.

The yeast in the dough does not replace the effort of the one who kneads; rather, it is a force which prolongs and makes his work fruitful. If, from the beginning, we look at interior graces in this way, we shall avoid some little difficulties in our meditation on the *Castle*.

We must be even more realistic. As we begin to enter the Mansions which are properly called "mystical" (because in them the heart is deepened under the divine action), we should understand that they are not a domain reserved to people who themselves wish to be "interior souls." God has to open it to all; otherwise, the Christian law cannot be accomplished. This follows from the First Commandment.

Because it is a commandment, it is theological and cannot be observed in all its perfection simply under the guidance of reason, aided by ordinary grace. In order to be completely faithful, we must not only deny and restrain ourselves, but launch out into a sphere that is beyond us. To do this, we need impulses which are proportionate to such a movement.

A great mistake Christians make is to look at the practice of this precept from the same angle as they do the other precepts. We think we have done enough if we practice it in a negative manner by avoiding what is contrary to it. But this minimum does not fulfill the law; besides, as St. Paul points out, this law is so vast that we are always in debt regarding it (see Rom 13, 8). In context he is speaking of the love of neighbor, but this love is one with the love of God and is formed in the same way.

Whether it be a question of our immediate neighbor or the brotherhood of all men, if we are to love with a love that is just and true, a transformation in the depths of our being such as St. Teresa begs for is necessary: "Force yourself to be such that you may be useful." Unless we realize this, there can be no efficacious zeal, no union that merits the name.

We are forced to conclude from our insufficiency in this area that we have an indispensable need for "particular assistance," and that because it is so necessary, it will not be lacking to anyone who is willing to deserve it through his own labor. "Give, and it shall be given to you" (Lk 6, 38). It is understood

that the basis is still the interior, resolute, persevering search of
the Second Mansions.

In the following Mansions, there is poured out that "good
measure, pressed down . . . running over" (Lk 6, 38), that gives
assurance and vigor and genuine exuberance to the Christian
life.

We must insist that the question here is one of the Christian
life, and that, in what concerns the essential aspects of this life,
the promise is for all. What makes the difference among Christians is their individual dispositions.

Religious life creates a very favorable situation, but those
who are called to it still bear their full responsibility. Like others, they too may not understand the Teresian teaching completely; they may give only imperfect answers to grace, which
will not occasion divine action. It may well happen that a giving which is more interior, although unperceived, in persons in
the world, may open the way to true life more fully.

Thus, in traversing the Mansions of the *Castle*, we must keep
in mind not only those who are really conscious of being disciples of St. Teresa, but also all the authentic members of the
family of Christ.

Clearly the finger of God must touch the secret of our powers
in order to provoke their hidden energies with a view to the act
they have to make, for they cannot discover it by themselves.
This act will consecrate the substance of our being by communicating to it the form of Christ.

How can this be done? It would seem we can give the answer
of the angel to the holy Virgin: "The power of the most High
will overshadow you" (Lk 1, 35); this "power" adapts itself to
the weakness of his creatures and does not come upon them
like suddenly turning on the light. They are not yet strong
enough for that. Hence, the "power" will lead them at first as
one leads the blind, by the senses that do not see: taste, smell,
hearing, touch.

Scripture gives us to understand that "Taste and see" (Ps 34, 8) means to learn through *taste* how to recognize the Lord. We are invited to run to him, drawn by the odor of his perfume (see Cant. 1:3–4).

Hearing has its own great share, primarily through faith— "Faith comes from what is heard" (Rom 10, 17)—but also through docility to the Lord when he makes himself present to the heart: "Hear, O daughter, consider, and incline your ear" (Ps 45, 10): "Let me hear what God the Lord will speak" (Ps 85, 8).

Then there is the sense of *touch*: "As one whom his mother comforts . . ." (Is 66, 13): "O that his left hand were under my head" (Cant. 8:3): "No one can come to me unless the Father . . . draws him" (John 6, 44); "O that you would kiss me with the kisses of your mouth" (Cant. 1:1).

All these things are connected with sensibility from within and tend to return to it. The power of the light is too much for this sensibility. To raise it up, it must be met on its own humble level. The light offers itself as a gentle attraction, a forceful persuasion, an effective gesture.

For, while the rudimentary impressions of taste and smell result in only an attraction, hearing gives entrance to more definite appeals and makes a decision possible, while the pressure of the divine hand produces the highest effects.

These are three progressive aspects of the "particular assistance" which will appear successively in the Fourth, Fifth and Sixth Mansions. Today's mentality ought to grasp easily the admirable fitness of these tactics. It knows what the subconscious is and how our acts spring in great part from a current of life which is deeper than our explicit intentions. This current is the ensemble of our natural and acquired tendencies, and we can neither reveal it clearly nor guide it directly.[2] Consequently, when a Christian wants to elevate himself, he is held back and finds it impossible to liberate his entire will.

Our subconscious life is not bad in itself, but it lies close to our instincts and is heavy with old habits, and consequently is the citadel of the "old man." Thus, it supports that duality about which St. Paul groans.

The very best psychology can do no better than discern the human causes of this division and put our freedom on guard. But, if his child is faithful, the Lord can and will penetrate into his automatic reactions, capture them and assimilate instinct itself. Then everything becomes more simple and the soul begins to possess itself in a unified way.

At this point, the human being realizes his beauty and his power; his power, which is the power of choosing God; his beauty, which is the harmony of his whole being as a result of his choice. The refusal to choose self has served as the opening. Under the divine action, ever more extended, this opening will grow larger, until the psyche is finally wide open to its divine Object without any risk of closing in again on self—which is heaven.

It is this eternal life which develops all through the different Mansions by the meeting of the one who kneads with the One who gives the leaven; a work imperceptible at first, then more and more efficacious, until the whole mass begins to rise.

NOTES

1. *Life,* Chap. xiv, *Collected Works of St. Teresa of Avila* vol I trans. by Kieran Kavanaugh O.C.D., and Otilio Rodriguez O.C.D., Washington, D.C., ICS Publications: 1976.
2. St. Teresa was not explicitly acquainted with this subterranean "self," but she seems to suppose it when she speaks for example, of graces acting directly on the will, or received in a certainty that is full of obscurity. Besides, her thought is much clarified in this modern light.

IX
The Sower

We like to picture the Fourth Mansions as a first degree of intimacy in which we can dream of establishing ourselves. It is a permissible dream, it seems, because, on the one hand, this degree is common enough—St. Teresa says so; and, on the other, there is reason to think that these Mansions can satisfy a good Christian. Does not the Saint describe them in terms which are full of esteem?

But this is not St. Teresa's idea at all. Weigh her words and you will see that, according to her, these Mansions are a place of transition: they are the preparation for the Fifth and cannot constitute an end in themselves. Hence, the question is not one of resting in the tranquility that seems to characterize them, but of grasping the real meaning of this sweetness and of responding to it by going further. This is a somewhat delicate undertaking, for many reach this stage, but few go beyond it.

Let us have the courage to look at the concrete experience described by our Saint and see what God intends to accomplish in us in this Mansion and to what he urges us. Here the leaven enters into the dough. The senses within begin to awake; the first to do so is the humblest: the taste. St. Teresa speaks to us of "divine tastes."

Mothers know the power of sweets in education. So does the Lord; and it is a real education that he is undertaking. But here there is no question of sugared "consolation." St. Teresa is definite on this point: we are penetrating into something profound and substantial, although we are penetrating only through an experience of an elementary order.

What does this educative experience reveal? Something simple enough: the good taste of a food means that it is suitable for our organism, that it is something we can assimilate. In the same way, the spiritual "taste" reveals through its sweetness the connaturality through grace which exists between the Father in heaven and his children. In this relationship, we also perceive the divine transcendence of which the child of God has equal need.

In other words, the soul begins to be instructed and to learn three things in this sweetness: that God is *very near;* that he is *his own good;* and that this good is *beyond us.* We think we know this, but in reality we are ignorant of it in our heart of hearts as long as we have not received the spiritual leaven.

When we do receive the spiritual leaven, what happens? The will seems to discover its real self; touched by God, it perceives in an obscure way the objective tendency hidden within—a dormant tendency, a paralyzed function. The yeast of the divine tastes is like a vitamin for it. Then this mysterious depth seems to awaken with great gentleness, a presentiment of equilibrium and harmony. Is all this not simply the Teresian "quiet," which is the second aspect of the divine action in the Fourth Mansions?

Like all happy dreams, this dream is euphoric and at the same time a call to life. There is a secret impetus in the very presentiment. The active element is scarcely visible, but nevertheless it is essential. It gives the divine action its true meaning. God wishes that his child make progress; to do that he must act.

Why may this call to action pass unperceived? Is it because it is so subtly intermingled with the tranquility whose charm fills the foreground? Perhaps most of all it is because the delight of

"quiet" is itself its dynamism: through it the soul impercepti-
bly escapes from supporting itself and passes on to the feeling
of an equilibrium which is offered from above "self."

The "quiet" is given to the soul to be a lever. It makes possible a maneuver which had seemed beyond its strength: the
decision to break with "self," which is the condition of the
objective parting. This experience is sufficient to make such a
rupture no longer seem a paradox. Touched, as we have said,
however lightly by God, the will can turn itself toward him
with ease, and beholding him, forget to see the abyss which
must be crossed.

"How can this be?"

"The power of the Most High will overshadow you."

"Let it be done to me . . ."

Is not all this the divine tactic, which we have glimpsed
before, now beginning to show itself? St. Teresa suggests this,
and at the same time lets us understand that at this point the
divine action is exceedingly secret.

It is important that the child of God shoulder *his* act in a
completely spontaneous manner. We must not forget that the
goal to be attained is an attitude of *will*: something that must be
rigorously free in order to be authentic. Even the supernatural
attraction must not be the determining factor in the strict sense.

So now we have the poor will, always more or less abused by
its good intentions, meeting a gentle hand which sets it on the
right road by sweetly humbling it. But the action is a restrained
one, for here God can permit himself only shy tendernesses. So
the soul experiences suspense, afraid that the gift offered it
from on high may escape it, because the One who is drawing it
holds himself back so as scarcely to touch it.

Nevertheless, it is already a divine work. Only God can reach
the will in its substance, revealing to it its grandeur and putting
it on its way. Through this gentle working, the essential task of

the soul is outlined and begins to become more deeply in-grained. The soul savors its delight to be sure, but it has a quite different task: without knowing how, it is learning to lose itself.

So the quiet leads to action. However hidden it may be, if it is a call, it needs an answer; if it is an impulse, it must be fol-lowed; if it is an education, the pupil must collaborate—and not by halves. This is the critical point. We have seen that the first ascent was rugged. Now a stage of interior sweetness pre-sents itself. What a temptation it may be to see in it a reward to be enjoyed, a repose to be prolonged, even thinking that perhaps we are touching the goal.

Elias had that experience under the juniper tree in the desert. An angel came to give him strength for a long journey, offered him bread, and brought him a gourd of the water that was always so precious in that arid country. The prophet ate and drank and, so say the Scriptures, fell asleep. The angel was not troubled. He gave him a second ration. Then, valiantly, the man of God resumed his journey (see 1 Kgs 19, 4–8).

Thus, the Lord has compassion on those he draws. He knows very well that their sensibility has not been converted and can only let itself be stopped by self. He knows too that this sensi-bility has been frustrated in its first attempts at pure renuncia-tion and that it instinctively reclaims its share of things. He accepts the fact that the soul does not see from the first the new work to be done. Yet, it must come to this knowledge or there will be no progress.

St. Teresa warns us of this. She knows that it often happens that, because of this lack of consciousness, the divine advances in the Fourth Mansions do not bear their fruit. She is ac-quainted with those ill-advised people who do not know how to draw profit from the visits of the Lord, and that these visits then become rare.

The sower goes out to sow the seed (see Lk 8,5). But are we not like the birds on the path of the sower, birds who take the seed only to feed upon it? Will we know how to be open land and deep soil in which the seed can bury itself and grow?

X

The Good Earth

When God deigns to call the most intimate depths of a soul to himself, in its turn that soul must give itself at the same depth; in other words, it must practice the art of leaving self on a new and more exacting level.

Do we really comprehend that? Probably not always. We have a tendency to think that the gift of God should expand and not despoil, and from this comes a subtle refusal. It is the hazard of the Fourth Mansions.

Let us follow St. Teresa and try to understand her better. She is speaking here of "tastes" and of "quiet," it is true, but she does not stop with these. Her final words ask for a special renouncement which she calls "humility."[1]

Humility in itself is nothing new; but what she is proposing here is a more interior form of humility, and laboring to acquire it is the special work proper to those whom God is beginning to visit.

In explaining this humility, she compares the divine action to that of a seal impressed upon wax. "The wax does not impress itself; it is only prepared for the impress: That is, it is soft, and it does not even soften itself, so as to be prepared; it merely remains quiet and offers no resistance."[2]

Someone will ask: Is this an active cooperation, a work? Most certainly it is; it takes a great deal of energy to remain quiet when one's sensibility is agitated. And "to offer no resistance" means in actual fact, repressing the resistances which are in us. It is a work which takes courage and skill. Here, more than ever, any straining of the will is a false maneuver, since the work must be done in the center of ourselves where the will is not mistress. Our only activity is to renounce our dependence on self, so that, like the wax, we may receive the impression.

Above all, it involves candor and compliance. Such is the kind of humility our spiritual mistress requires at this time. She says that, for a soul favored with "divine tastes," humility consists not only in thinking itself unworthy of them, but of doing nothing to attain them.[3] It is indeed the *quiet* attitude.

This attitude has as its foundation not only considerations of modesty and delicacy, but a more elevated motive which the Saint puts in first place: "The most essential thing is that we should love God without any motive of self-interest."[4]

A little further on she says: "The soul must leave itself in the hands of God ... completely disregarding its own advantage."[5] And again: "The most important and pleasing thing in God's eyes is our remembering his honor and glory and forgetting ourselves and our own profit and ease and pleasure."[6]

Our work is always that of renunciation, but now in a way that is more worthy of God, for it involves the abandonment of a more precious good: we part company with ourselves on an entirely interior level, that is on the level of the graces received. It is precisely the answer which these graces demand.

To receive everything without trying to hold on to anything is the way to receive much and to give everything back to God. Consequently, the graces of the Fourth Mansion bring forth their fruit through the simple fact that, by remaining in this humble quiet, the soul "lets itself be marked without offering any resistance." When we receive a grace in order to delight in it, or covet it in order to retain its sweetness, we mistake the very meaning of this grace.

It is so easy to have just this misconception: St. Teresa points out some indications of this:

—to be eager to procure these "tastes" by this or that superficial means[7];
—to take advantage of these in order to judge others[8];
—to be afflicted if these are not given us to our heart's content.[9]

These are three false attitudes which do not permit the divine seed to germinate. It has fallen on soil which is too shallow, or which is encumbered with an undergrowth of egoism.

The good earth is the "good and perfect" heart, which receives all into its depth and covets nothing. There the grain is safe indeed. We do not busy ourselves with looking at it or feeling it. It can lead its fruitful life.

To bear fruit, to live its life—what do these mean with regard to the divine sowing? The fruit and the life of every supernatural operation is charity. From this time on, then, it is a question of love; not yet of perfect love, but of a beginning which, if it is to be authentic, must have to some degree the form and perfume of love.

Here St. Teresa lays down her great principle: "The important thing . . . is to love much."[10] Then, as if anxious about what she had just said and about the misunderstandings it could arouse, she makes her meaning more precise: "Perhaps we do not know what love is . . . for love consists not in the extent of our happiness, but in the firmness of our determination to try to please God in everything."[11] Now we are on the solid ground of piety, far from the false appetites noted above.

The graces received at this point are a preparation for the following Mansions. Our goal, which is the union of the will, is adherence in act. The whole work of the moment is to let ourselves be put on the road of this act. But why not gather the joy which presents itself and which is the gift of God? Why so much caution? The answer is simple: joy is a fruit and we are only at the season of blossom. Pick a bud in spring and you suppress its fruit. Much respect must be shown to the first sprouts of the season.

Therefore, we need to know how to savor in a reserved manner the first advances of the Lord, to respect his springtime. This very reserve is a sign that the divine action is real and that the soul is receiving it to the full. Perhaps a comparison will help us to understand this.

Who has not seen jelly being made? To try the syrup you let a drop fall into a glass of cold water. If it is at the proper temperature, the drop goes right to the bottom of the glass and quickly comes up again in the shape of a pearl.

It is the same with spiritual sweetness. While weak it stays on the surface of the soul or is diluted in sensibility. When it has become strong and truly divine, it goes down to the depths, and if it finds purity and freshness there, it comes up again, drawing the most secret forces of the will with it. This is the dynamism proper to the Fourth Mansions.

The creature's whole action is this purity, this candor which keeps the divine gift present and thereby makes it cooperative. This is an "immobile" action but nonetheless a real one, an action of love, which far from hoarding the gift for itself, puts itself at love's service. We should pay great attention to this point, for it is an orientation which will decide the future. It is a question of choosing or of refusing the way of life in "spirit."

We are so tied to matter that unconsciously we carry over material instincts into what we call spiritual life, and in so doing we falsify it. The life of the flesh is to covet and to absorb; that of the spirit is to leave oneself and to give oneself. It is the flesh that decrees that all renunciation is an impoverishment and poverty a decadence. The spirit, on the contrary, makes its fortune when it loses itself. Forgetfulness of its own advantages is its business, its privilege, and its nobility.

So, to desire interior sweetness *for itself* is to desire according to the flesh and to render that sweetness sterile. A formal resistance occurs: the opposition of flesh to the spirit. There is no ambiguity in St. Paul's requirement: "If we live by the spirit, let us also walk by the spirit" (Gal 5, 25). And again: "If by the spirit you put to death the deeds of the body, you will live" (Rom 8, 13). In the present case the actions of the flesh are the desires of selfish sensibility.

The true life which ought to develop in the course of the following mansions, therefore, depends on the direction taken in these. How serious a thing it is and yet, perhaps, how rarely understood!

The Lord has many children who are his in principle and who, on hearing these things, desire to be so completely. Unfortunately, the reality escapes them—this total intimacy with God—because they have not chosen poverty of spirit. For, the Apostle says again: "all who are led by the Spirit of God are *sons of God*" (Rom 8, 14). Only these, not others; the title is incommunicable.

The poor in spirit are immediately treated as true children. "If we achieve true detachment," says St. Teresa, "the Lord will not fail to grant us this favor [of 'quiet'], and many others which we shall not even know how to desire."[12]

If we want to be warmed by the sun, it is enough to keep ourselves in its orbit. He whose only concern is to "please God" lives in the orbit of love, exposed to its rays. On the contrary, he who seeks himself, even from pious motives, is like a planet which gets lost and grows cold. Or, if you would like another image, the star which shines is the one which does not cease to consume itself. How numerous they are, perhaps, those pale stars, which will never reach their true light in this life because

they do not understand to what a point they must give themselves over to the fire in order to be able to shine out in splendor.

Here indeed is the word of the Gospel verified: "Seek first his
kingdom and his righteousness, and all these things shall be
yours as well" (Mt 6, 33).

Thus, we see a passage in which everything hinges on subtle
differences, which require a great sensitiveness. The result may
appear modest: not even an act, only a simple attitude. But this
first consent, however light it may be, is decisive, for it is
enough to tip the balance of the heart, to incline it toward the
place where God is awaiting it.

NOTES

1. "Practice what I advised in the preceding mansions,
   then—humility, humility! for God lets himself be van-
   quished by this and grants us all we ask" (IV, 2:8).
2. This comparison is found in the chapters devoted to the
   Fifth Mansions; it is related to the Fourth Mansions inas-
   much as it pertains to a preparation (see V, 2:13, Peers). *The
   Complete Works of Saint Teresa of Jesus*, trans. by E. Allison Peers New York: Sheed and Ward. 1946)
3. IV, 2:8.
4. IV, 2:8, Peers.
5. IV, 3:6, Peers.
6. IV, 3:6, Peers.
7. "Though we may meditate and try our hardest, and though
   we shed tears to gain it, we cannot make this water flow"
   (IV, 2:8).
8. III, 2:19.

9. "They cannot patiently endure to be shut out from entering the presence of our King" (III, 1:10).

10. IV, 1:8, Peers.

11. IV, 1:8, Peers.

12. IV, 2:8, Peers.

FIFTH MANSIONS

The Fifth Mansions are a first degree of union with God, fruit of the graces of the Fourth. St. Teresa calls this degree "union of the will." It is a stage which deserves great attention, for, as the Saint makes clear, on the one hand it is accessible to every Christian who is truly willing to give himself, and on the other it is normally the introduction to the very special graces of the following Mansions.

XI
May Your Will be Mine!

As St. Teresa begins to treat of the Fifth Mansions, she exclaims: "Oh my Sisters, how shall I describe the riches, the treasures and the joys contained in [these] Mansions. Would it not be better to say nothing about them?"[1]

Happily she was not silent. She is going to show us what union[2] with God is so that we may learn how to attain it. There are so many vague ideas, so many misunderstandings, about "union." Usually, it is seen as a mystery which takes place in the domain of the emotions: as sweetnesses and intimacies whose nature we do not understand, but which, at least hypothetically, are situated beyond the ordinary level of "good Christians." Or, from a more modest point of view, an experience of the supernatural or any somewhat ardent feeling is called a "grace of union." In a broad sense, all who are recollected and watchful in their efforts to please God are considered as "united to him."

These are not the ideas we are going to consider. Union is not a feeling; it is a solid psychological reality. It is high reality, for it places the soul in a relationship with the divine life which is both very close and at the same time very definite.

We must not stop at this. "Fear not, little flock," said Jesus, "for it is your Father's good pleasure to give you the Kingdom" (Lk 12, 32). The Kingdom for which God destines us is none other than his own life of love. Let us believe the Lord, and try

to find out how we can participate in this life, busying ourselves with what makes up the *substance* of union of the will.
Proceeding in this manner, there is no danger of illusion; there
is no problem about what we can see or feel under the influence
of an accidental "favor." Rather, the question is one of a fact in
the development of our life of grace.

St. Teresa defines union of the will in a few words as "love
united to love."[3] Love—the pure movement of love that we
have named objective act and which we suppose to have been
attained here. In one leap of sovereign liberty, the soul disen-
gages itself from everything that could hold it captive so that it
may become this simple desire for God. This is the fact; by
grace it is possible, magnificently fulfilling human psychology.

In this movement, the will identifies itself with the act by
which God desires himself. That is the reason such a realization
merits the name of "union." The little creature become love
makes "one spirit" (1 Cor 6, 17) with Him who is Love.

Only one spirit—in a kind of participation in the aspiration
of love which is in God, associating the creature not with his
Being but with the divine act. Union is in the act; St. Teresa
compares it to two candles which mingle their flames without
being merged together.[4]

Nevertheless, it remains true that the act is life. One only act,
one only spirit means, then, one only life, the divine life, the
true life of the spirit. Such is the magnitude of union of the will.

It is too high an aspiration, too far away, we are tempted to
think. Are we really incapable of a dream of love that reaches
even to God? Do we not carry in the secret recesses of our being
a thirst for a "living water" that we have not yet encountered? If
we had more logical minds and more powerful hearts, perhaps
we would see to what that thirst leads, and would desire, at any
price, that act in which "love is united to love." Then we would
not say that it is too far away, for no being is closer to us than
our God: "We are of his race," and we do not live fully save in
sharing his life.

This pure movement of the will is something so positive according to St. Teresa that the soul always retains the certitude of having "been in God."[5] When the soul fulfills itself in this way, it cannot but be aware that what had been an obscure tendency within it has suddenly found its resting place. The arrow has reached the target. The questing bee is buried in the flower. And when a spirit has found such a place of rest beyond self, has it not found God himself?

The more the will has been searching, rejecting the tranquility even of nature, the better it will recognize God in this sign of pure transport and true rest. This perfect movement is of short duration, says St. Teresa. Here again, this is not surprising; it is the peak of a curve, a forceful beat. On earth, life does not stabilize itself in a strong beat, it also progresses by weak beats, as do all rhythms.

The summits of union will be brief and perhaps very rare. However, there is a climate of union which should remain. We can and ought to aspire to this "climate" from the beginning of our spiritual work.

In what does it consist? Again the Saint tells us. For her the idea of habitual union reduces itself to that of "conformity": "following the will of God in all things."[6] According to her, this disposition is both the sufficient condition and the substance of union.

Its condition: "True union can always be attained, by forcing ourselves to renounce our own will and by following the will of God in all things."

Its substance: "I can only declare . . . that, if this be the case, we have already obtained union with God." The Saint then adds, developing her thought carefully: do not be anxious "for that other delectable union I have spoken of, for the most valuable thing about it is that it proceeds from this union which I am now describing . . . ; *we cannot attain to the [first] if we are not sure that we have the union in which we resign our wills to the will of God."*[7]

We can note in passing that here we see the well-established harmony between the strong beat and the weak beat of union.

When we read this text, does not "habitual" union seem something very simple? Yes, without doubt; but perhaps not quite in the way we understand. Regarding this "conformity" which she declares to be the union itself, St. Teresa defines her thought in words which are somewhat mysterious: "Provided that the union be real."[8]

What does she mean? Perhaps this: there is a conformity which, however excellent it may be, does not, cannot, go as far as union. It consists simply in making oneself pliant in adapting oneself to the things that God wills or permits. It is what we ordinarily call being united to the will of God. However, this effort, although indispensable and of great worth, is not on the same plane as union, for the very simple reason that it does not bind the will to God himself, but only to his decrees.

This remark is important, not to discourage people who are on so excellent a road, but to avoid a misunderstanding that would distort the teaching of St. Teresa. This misunderstanding could be frequent in circles where fervor is cultivated along with some distrust (that is, some lack of comprehension) of the "mystical." It is so easy to design a master plan of spirituality under the heading of fidelity and abandonment, and, for the comfort of impatient hearts, to call the moral attitude thus formed, "union." This union is not "real," rather it is intentional. What then will turn conformity into a *real* climate for union? The Saint demands submission in the spirit, one that is totally interior, not only desiring every event willed by God, but desiring only God above every event. It involves willing in the way in which he himself wills: "What do you think is his will? ... That we ... be made one with him and with his Father."[9]

Something more than a mere nuance can be found here; a great distance exists between the virtuous exercise of the will

and its true act. This act is a mystery; it is very near to the
divine act. On account of its perfection, it demands a special
grace, as we shall see, for "every perfect gift is from above" (Jas
1, 17).

In spite of that, it remains very human. Our will is first of all
created, then predestined for such an act: created, because its
natural function is to "choose God"; predestined, because
supernatural life is properly to choose God in God and as God.
"May your will be mine!" So it is in this perfect will.

Union of the will, therefore, is a normal thing, desired by God
for everyone. When we realize this fact, we see our vocation as
baptized Christians in its true perspective, one which reveals
both its amplitude and our consequent responsibilities. Furthermore, there is a reality in this way of conceiving union
which is especially adapted to souls of today who are avid for
all that concerns "being" in its depth. Consequently, it depends
on our sincerity and our courage whether this grace is to enter
our lives.

Certainly this is the thought of the holy Mother when she
says: God "requires no impossibilities from anyone in order to
gain these riches."[10] "The little we can do will hardly have
been accomplished, when this insignificant work of ours will
be united by God to his greatness."[11]

Achievement, work, and union of the will result from the
preparations of the heart in the same way as the harvest follows
the tilling of the soil. Although God must intervene, nevertheless it remains a normal consequence, with the logical rigor of
effect following cause, of a decision which we ourselves make.

At this central point of the spiritual life, where the Lord
enters more clearly into the scene, he does not intend to
supplant the initiative of his little creature. On the contrary, he
asks us to play for high stakes and to involve ourselves fully. St.
Teresa insists on this point of our responsibilities: few of us
prepare ourselves "that our Lord may reveal this jewel to us!"[12]

"We fall far short of what must be done in order to obtain perfect conformity with the will of God."[13]

It should be made clear here that such a disposition is essentially different from voluntarism; the latter results entirely from the human tension within the will. The Saint does not ask for spectacular efforts and performances. For her, the will is the faculty which gives—gives itself. To attain to this genuine, deep gift is no small thing; it is the will's vocation and, in its essence, constitutes "union of will." In the *Interior Castle*, there will always be the problem in one form or another, of a work to be done, a response to be made, a fidelity to be strengthened, but always, and especially, of a movement of the heart: of love and humility.

The logical consequence of making a start demands that we tend toward union. For want of understanding what it is, we may look for union in the wrong way; for want of courage, we do not achieve it.

We are not, then, being presumptuous when we meditate on this subject. Rather, doing so gives us an occasion to practice humility. If these Mansions are not opening to us after a sufficiently long time, it is because, in spite of our "good desire," we are holding back before grace. Indeed, if the Lord has not taken us by the hand, it is because something in us does not want his grasp, for he said: "Him who comes to me I will not cast out" (Jn 6, 37).

This quotation is of great, practical importance. Doubtless it would be wrong to present union as directly accessible to our efforts; yet, it would be a greater error to expect it to come from the divine pleasure as a "favor," pure and simple. We must understand that it is offered to us as a duty that is linked to the fulfillment of our more simple duties. Light can be shed on these small tasks when we look at union in this way.

In what, then, does this spiritual duty consist, this "disposition" of which St. Teresa speaks, this movement by which the

Christian "comes to God?" Through and above the work of the virtues—which are always indispensable—it consists in saying a genuine "yes" to grace. This "yes" is the profound result of an objective effort, a humble but well-hidden victory. The Lord calls us to great things only through deeds equal to our capacity.

But it is a "yes" which is very exacting. As St. Teresa comments: God "would have you *keep back nothing*. He will *have it all* for himself, and according to what . . . you know yourself to have given, the favors he will grant you will be small or great."[14] You see what the Saint considers to be the extent of our responsibility in regard to the Fifth Mansions.

She adds to this declaration: "There is no better test than this of whether or not our prayer attains to union." A precious formula; in the practical sphere it is the answer to our question: "What is union of the will?" From our point of view, it is simply the culminating point of the gift of self.[15]

With this criterion, we can distinguish it from what may resemble it. Because it is fulfillment, we must not confuse it with impressions or emotions; because it is total gift, it is something quite other than the Fourth Mansions, where the soul has still to learn this gift.

NOTES

1. v, 1:1.
2. We would have liked to avoid the word "union," which only too commonly brings to mind an experience of feeling. At least we shall try hard to circumscribe its meaning.
3. v, 4:1.
4. See vii, 2:5.

5. "God visits the soul in a manner which prevents its doubting . . . that he was within it and that it dwelt in him" (v, 1:8, Peers).
6. v, 3:3.
7. v, 3:3, Peers.
8. v, 1:6.
9. v, 3:7.
10. v, 1:2.
11. v, 2:4.
12. v, 1:2.
13. v, 3:6.
14. v, 1:3, Peers.
15. We must not forget that, in St. Teresa's thought, the will is the energy by which the soul *gives itself.* Consequently, its perfect act is a perfect gift.

XII
To the Mountain of the Lord

We have just seen that union of the will is not a simple "favor," but the normal way to our being present to God. Thus, every Christian has the duty to dispose himself for it; he does so unconsciously whenever he is completely sincere.

God looks for adorers "in spirit and in truth". The gift of the will which leads to real union is the concrete expression of this worship.

Hence, this chapter will have a completely practical end: to search out the way of arriving surely at union. St. Teresa tells us that the way is open to *all*. "Our business," she writes, "is to practice the virtues and to submit our wills in all things to the will of God . . . not to wish that *our* will may be done, but *his.*"[1]

There are three stages to this: the first is supposed to be attained as much by the virtuous effort of the Second and Third Mansions as by correspondence to the grace of the Fourth.

The second is the conformity we considered in the preceding chapter. It does not go so far as to achieve true union of the will, but it is a progressing toward this goal.

The third represents total conformity; it is the immediate preparation. It makes us feel the force of the negative instruction: not to wish that our will be done.

The will reaches the limit of its submission and the peak of its power only at the moment in which it denies itself. At this point it goes beyond the dispositions of fidelity and abandonment in the ordinary sense of these words. The strength and the extent of this denial far exceed simple fidelity; the decision here is more spontaneous than simple abandonment.

This characteristic of energetic liberty is essential to the Fifth Mansions. St. Teresa compares them to the flight of the butterfly which has emerged from its cocoon. We have been talking about renunciation from the very beginning of our meditations on the *Castle*. Now, renunciation must produce its effects, and thus become complete. It is the story of the silkworm enclosing itself in the prison that it spins for itself. "It is necessary that the worm die,"² the Saint repeats more than once.

Many things must die in us in order to make room for divine life. In several passages of her works, Teresa points out what tastes, needs, habits, affections and expectations must be sacrificed. She especially demands our relentless pursuit of what she calls "honor." In this word she sums up the arbitrary demands of our human personality.

Our yes or no before such a sacrifice is crucial at this point, for what is at stake is the handing over of the very center of our heart. "Not to wish that our will be done" is a formula which is inexorable in its clarity. It shows us that our task here is not to build but to *dig* until this center is reached and surrendered. Yes, says the author of the *Castle*, it is necessary to "dig without respite,"³ for the grace of union is a "treasure hidden within us." We must understand the situation: the roots of the will, which should be united to God, hide themselves. They disguise themselves under all kinds of sentiments that seem highly virtuous. The problem is to find them and to wrest them from the grasp of "self."

This energetic, negative work is not a simple destroying. The symbol of the silkworm itself suggests something quite different. "Let the silkworm die!" exclaims St. Teresa. In reality it does not die at all; it only abandons a certain mode of existence. It stops that it may concentrate itself in itself in order to discover and unfold its real life. It does not even suffer when it shrinks itself into its cocoon, for it follows an instinct of growth.

It would be the same for us if, from the beginning, we understood the laws of progress and did not let the passion for returning to self pervert even our understanding. For we carry deep within us as a vital need an "objective sense," whose first flowering constitutes union of the will. We possess it as the perfect seed of our honor and true joy. We have wings within us. For these to develop and open, we will have to give of our substance like the silkworm; only we will have to suffer more than it does, for we have to transform deformation.

Such an effort is of prime importance at this point and reveals its positive value when it affects the center of the will. In the measure that the soul learns to forget itself, it feels springing up within it the forces of life which draw it joyously along to perfect forgetfulness.

We would be living in a dream world if we failed to understand this positive element of the road to union. St. Teresa emphasizes it in an admirable manner. Certainly she demands an ascent in abnegation: we shall not go on to union, she declares, except by "taking away from ourselves and by giving of ourselves."[4] Yet, like a real mother, to achieve this she offers us something besides a vertical ascent along the path of the "nothing." She has her secret for making us climb without getting dizzy, a secret inspired by St. Paul, St. John and the Gospel. It may not seem very original, but when we scrutinize it, we shall see how profound it is because it is so practical.

The secret is the perfect love of neighbor: "In proportion as you advance in fraternal charity, you are increasing in your love of God"[5]; "The way to know whether we love God is to see whether we love our neighbor or no."[6]

Is not this what the Lord teaches when he declares that the Second Commandment is like to the First? Union with God is linked to union with neighbor like a musical resonance: two chords, one of which evokes the other by vibrating: the neighbor so near us is the door to the highest love. This is the way Christ appears to us in his passion. All is for the glory of his Father and for the work of redemption; yet, from reading the Gospel, one would say he was solely occupied with those around him.

He heals Malchus, he entreats Judas, he assures the safety of his Apostles, he turns toward Peter at the decisive moment, he offers Pilate a ray of light. We see his solicitude for the women of Jerusalem, for his executioners, for his Mother and St. John, and, at the last moment, the promise to the Good Thief. Through these creatures, who are near him, he carries on his great life as Savior.

These are the principles. Now let us ask the Saint *how* we must love our neighbor. Her answer is very simple: "By works." And she indicates these works: "Our Lord expects works from us! If you see a sick sister whom you can relieve, never fear of losing your devotion; compassionate her; if she is in pain, pity her, and when there is need, fast so that she may eat, not so much for her sake, as because you know your Lord asks it of you.

"If someone else is well spoken of in your presence, be more pleased than if it were yourself.

"It is a great good to rejoice at your sister's virtues being known, and to feel as sorry for the fault you see in her, as if it were your own, hiding it from the sight of others."[7]

"If you constrain yourselves and force your will, as far as possible, to comply in all things with your sisters' wishes, although sometimes you may lose your own rights by doing so; if you forget your self-interests for theirs, however much nature may rebel; if, when there is an opportunity, you take some burden upon yourself to ease your neighbor of it, he will give you more that you know how to desire."[8]

This is the manner in which we are to love, although there

are nuances, degrees, and stresses in this program which we must note.

First of all, Teresa sets aside everything that could be too emotional in our attention or compassion toward others by fixing the motive of our charitable act: "... not so much for her sake, as because you know your Lord asks it of you." Such a motive rules out natural complacency and superficial amiability, and more or less affected eagerness.

Only strong, earnest self-sacrifice is left—again with a special mark. Although the Saint does not exclude diligence in rendering service or in comforting or giving pleasure, her accent is on the *interior* quality of the charity, itself measured by the amount of abnegation demanded in the way of corporal privations and of renunciations in the moral order. Concerning these latter Teresa willingly goes into detail: loving the honor of our sisters more than our own; appreciating their virtues; hiding their faults; finding joy in their success; content to be deprived of our own rights for their sake; forgetting our interests for theirs; making our own will yield for love of another's will.

Notice that what is prescribed in every line of this program is from the perspective of abasing one's own personality for the benefit of others.

We are at the heart of the Teresian strategy. Within the very simple framework of daily life, the holy Mother offers us in a few unpretentious words a way of great fraternal thoughtfulness. Such thoughtfulness exacts profound sacrifices; it is an "abyss" for "self" and its pretensions. But on this road of love the obstacles topple before love.

Indeed, how can the necessary condition of "no longer desiring our own will" be realized more concretely or more surely than in this affective renunciation? The "nothing" of St. John of the Cross is entering into the will in its vigorous and luminous form, since it is for the joy of others. The gift of the will is becoming more real and complete.

There is scarcely any human compensation for the sacrifices on which such love lives. What is left when one consents, on every occasion, to losing the support of his earthly equilibrium: his autonomy, reputation and every right?

When all is welcomed with the inward dispositions that Teresa wishes, the soul is established at the threshold of true union, both by the depth of abnegation that is formed in this exercise and by the quality of the love to which it invites and which, sooner or later, grace will offer.

To understand this better, let us imagine one of those small incidents which are always possible in our contacts with others: a little story told about us by a companion. There is no conscious malice, but the speaker's zeal is not very enlightened, his earnestness a little impassioned, and the result: conviction in him, some reserve and coolness in us.

What should our reaction be? Accept the story with resignation, murmuring: "Oh! It is nothing!"? This may seem sublime, but there is something better: to love the little human joy of our neighbor, to be happy to reward him with a gift that comes from within ourself. The Saint asks nothing less. And if we try it, grace is there to make of this little effort an immense act.

Fraternal love is transfigured when it is thus completely adopted; it becomes very pure and is one with "God's love [that] has been poured into our hearts through the Holy Spirit" (Rom 5, 5), which is the communication of love itself. So, by an unpretentious path and, as St. John of the Cross would say, "in a dark night" the soul, all unobserved, goes "out" from virtuous effort to enter into a new world.

Supported by all that it learned by living the preceding Mansions to the full, and through its initiation into fraternal charity, this soul has chosen to exchange the petty life of its own heart with the life of the spirit of love, finding in this choice a "taste of eternal life."[9]

Now it no longer has to cultivate renunciation in order to go "where it knows not." It grasps with both hands the good it has been seeking. "He who has found love," says the *Imitation,* "has found a good above all goods."[10]

In this new region of the gift of self, the little heroisms of charity no longer seem like deprivations, but rather like debts of justice which it is sweet to satisfy: justice toward God in disdaining one's human rights in exchange for such a good; justice toward oneself in choosing the best and not lingering on anything else; justice toward him who is weaker by abandoning to him with a full heart whatever can help him exist while he awaits better things. This is the "royal road," the highest liberty, conformity according to the spirit, for it can well be said—following the style of St. Francis de Sales—that to give the will of our heart is to give the heart of our will.

In summary, we might say that, through the goodness of God, the will has found the key to "objectivity" in loving others.

But at this point another simple and radiant word presents itself, "innocence." When objective virtue has conquered the center of the heart, it produces this fruit. For innocence is the disposition of the heart to threaten no one and never to set itself up as a rival; it implies that it wishes nothing for itself. The covetous heart is not a quiet one.

Thus, innocence is a virtue of the heights. "Who shall ascend the [mountain] of the Lord? . . . He who has clean hands and a pure heart" (Ps 24, 3–4). It is also a sign of the encounter: God himself is innocence, goodness without complexity, without calculation, without limits. He has the eyes of a child. He looks for eyes like his in order to plunge his own into them. Is there not already union when there is the same gaze?

Furthermore, the promise of the psalm will be fulfilled: "With the innocent you will be innocent" (Ps 17, 26D). In this area of union, where the will keeps nothing back for itself, the Lord will no longer keep anything back for himself, and at the moment he chooses there will be a joyous surprise—not a solemn dialogue, but the wondrous meeting of two innocences.

The tiny act whose immense consequences we have just ex-

amined is only one type of a thousand others. We can never
emphasize enough that practical progress toward union of the
will is made by very delicate and very interior acts. Since union
is a vital reaction, it must be able to spring from the most
humble events. Thus, it is a matter of taking complete advantage of daily occasions. Unfortunately, these opportunities are
rarely understood or entirely accepted; for that reason the
decisive step is exceptional.

The act to be performed is simple, but who can measure its
extent?[11] It achieves what psychologists call the passage from
"self" to "others." It is not simply occasional; it supposes the
objective tendency of the spirit and therefore implies profound
preparations. St. Teresa says that he who has consented to as-
sume it will retain a beneficial longing for it.

Note that such an act can be styled heroic, not in the sense of
a flowery grandeur, but because it is a sure triumph of grace, for
Christian heroism is nothing other than the subordination of
the natural affections to the great life of charity.[12]

To meditate on the spiritual scope of the love of neighbor is
to enter deeply into St. Teresa's thought. "We love ourselves
too much," says the holy Mother, "and are too prudent to give
up any of our rights. What a deception! May God by his mercy
give us light lest we fall into such darkness!"[13]

NOTES

1. III, 2:8.
2. V, 2, 3.
3. V, 1.
4. V, 2.
5. V, 3:8.
6. V, 3:8–9.

7. v, 3:11.
8. v, 3:12.
9. The *Living Flame* of love, Strophe II. *Collected Works of St. John of the Cross*, trans. by Kieran Kavanaugh O.C.D. and Otilio Rodriquez, O.C.D., Washington, D.C. ICS Publications, 1973.
10. Bk. III, 5.
11. See on this subject the clear lines of Rev. Fr. Marie-Eugène O.C.D. in *I Am a Daughter of the Church* p. 183: " . . . the importance of acts in order to attain this union [of the will] . . . There must . . . acts and acts over again truly to develop charity . . . The development of charity and the union of the will that is its fruit are bound up with *imponderables*. One person goes along accomplishing his duty honestly . . . Another, his neighbor, differs little from him; but awakened fervor keeps on faithfully attentive to purify his intention and to add to his acts that little nothing which gives them their perfection: his acts are good and intense. The latter, and he alone, is growing in the virtue of love. Years pass in a life that the two lead in common and that differentiates them, but little exteriorly. And yet, the second attains at length to the prayer of union; while the first, the better endowed, perhaps, is lulled into an ease and routine that have arrested all progress." I am a Daughter of the Church, Fr. Marie-Eugène, O.C.D., translated by Sr. M. Verna Clare, C.S.C. Fides Publishers, Inc. Notre Dame, In. 1955
12. There is no question here of the heroism of a Joan of Arc, but of the heroism of *the interior act*; this can only be understood in the grace of an interior vocation that has been *duly cultivated*.
13. v, 4:4.

XIII
And It Will Be Opened to You

Love of others is the way that leads to that "innocence" which is the doorway to divine life. It is easily understood that this "innocence" sums up and crowns the serious work of abnegation which St. Teresa puts in the first place in treating of the Fifth Mansions. At the end of this road is union with God realized? It seems so, recalling certain of the Saint's statements: "In proportion to what you know you have given him, will your reward be great or small. There is no more certain sign whether or not we have reached the prayer of union."[1]

"True union can always be attained, with the help of divine grace, by forcing ourselves to renounce our own will and by following the will of God in all things . . . I can only declare, as I shall again and again, that if this be the case, we have already obtained union with God."[2]

"Our Lord asks but two things of us: love for him and for our neighbor. . . . Let us try to do his will perfectly, *then* we shall be united to him."[3]

But she also says: "The prayer of union is the 'cellar' in which our Lord sets us, *when and how he chooses*, but we cannot enter it through any effort of our own. His Majesty alone can bring us there."[4]

Is this a contradiction? Not at all. Everything becomes clear in the light of the Church's teaching on the development of charity. For really there is no question of anything else. What Teresa calls "union" is one stage of the development: the moment when, having gone beyond everything that is contrary to it, charity attains to its true life.

We must not forget that every new degree of this virtue is a gratuitous gift, a direct operation of the Holy Spirit. We do not attain any degree by our labor alone, even aided by grace.

"Knock and it will be opened to you," says the Gospel; Jesus does not say: "Knock and you will finish by breaking down the door," but, "it will be opened to you." If it pleases the Master, his servants will open it from within. The last lines of St. Teresa quoted above translate the meaning of this Gospel passage exactly. Moreover, the first words of this paragraph also correspond to the divine promise. For it is a promise to which God binds himself: "Knock, and *it will be opened to you.*"

There is certainly a relation of cause and effect between the virtuous work and the grace of union. Nevertheless, the work is not the real cause, although it does urge the divine cause with a kind of authority, because the Lord is faithful to his laws. St. Teresa expresses this in words which go right to the point: "Though we can take no active part in this work of God within us, yet we may do much to prepare ourselves to receive this grace, by putting ourselves in the requisite dispositions."[5]

Indeed, we see plainly that God himself is close by in this progress in our "dispositions." We understand too that, in the perfect gift of self, the Saint already perceives more than a disposition—even a sign of the grace of union secretly received. Whatever this transition may be, perceived or not, after having insisted on our responsibilities, we must now consider the fact that this union is a gratuitous gift. But why this gift? What is its meaning and its extent?

Without it we shall never be what we ought to be; we shall never do what we could do. Consciously or not, we shall vegetate. That is intolerable for God. Besides he is not stingy with this gift. But how can he communicate it to some one who cannot understand or welcome it?

Souls who understand their true end, who are tireless in pursuing it, who are wholly faithful to the elemental ideas of Christian life—these souls are rare, perhaps. Whoever does not live these elements fully, can only be left to his trade as a day laborer. Yet, this is not God's will, nor St. Teresa's dream. Only the grace of union realizes the full and direct movement of the will toward God which extends to forgetfulness of all other interests. Such a movement supposes that the will is seized by God himself even in its inmost parts.

We saw in the Fourth Mansions how the finger of God "touches" the interior of the soul ever so lightly, and leaves in it a longing for objectivity. Here it is not a "gentle touching"; it is sovereign energy which is offered and which penetrates; better still, a persuasive force,[6] for the Lord does not say: "If you are willing." He makes the soul will—will completely without any tension. This is a will received, a will from above.

Now it is no longer a question of taking our bearings, but of following divine guidance. Yet, let us repeat: union is on the normal road of the Christian life. Christian resources are powerful but exacting. Is not the baptismal character complete in itself? Is it not an insertion—nay more, an immersion—in Christ, an intombment of all that is not conformable to him? (see Col 2, 12). And is not the gift of the Holy Spirit in everyone who is confirmed an imperious demand? "He yearns jealously over the spirit which he has made to dwell in us" (Js 4, 5). He must have a response. God gives himself if we are disposed for it, and this is the grace of union—nothing less suffices; nothing less fulfills the Christian vocation.

This grace, then, is simply a sacramental effect. We were taught in catechism that these effects come at their proper hour, that they are often held in abeyance by the lack of the right dispositions. What a practical application we can make here! It is in fact and not by right that the children of God do not all speak the same language.[7] Does this point of view perhaps seem unusual? We are so accustomed to rank the graces of the

Fifth Mansions among the "mystical" phenomena which have nothing in common with ordinary life. It is necessary to maintain the sacramental aspects of these graces as of all the "mystical" gifts. They are not an ill-defined addition on the margin of the program. The normal ways of sanctification, through their own operation, procure the substance of these gifts and graces.

It is extremely important for us to consider this truth. Then we shall not think that it is presumptuous for us to aspire to this fulfillment. Instead of finding it normal to stand apart from it, we shall humble ourselves before it.

Baptism, Confirmation, Holy Communion—all contribute to the development of charity, which is itself the development of true "mystical" life. But most of these steps on the way to this life receive no special notice. Why give so much attention to the one we call "union"? Think of the comparison of the silkworm. In its cocoon it too passes through a series of transformations which no one sees. They are all interesting, but the one in which it breaks its cocoon and opens its wings is unique.

Likewise, in the life of charity, the ordinary law is that grace gives success to efforts. "She prospered him in his labors" (Wis 10, 10). But, there are more striking successes which do not lie within our field of labor; a great step is taken when, in the Lord's hour, he himself makes the words of Wisdon come true: "She increased the fruit of his toil" (*ibid.*).

What is it then that places this degree of union in a new order? At each degree, grace triumphs over such and such an obstacle; in this one, it inaugurates its proper life—something altogether new.

Imagine a skillful embroiderer who has been furnished with only soiled and tangled skeins. Her first work will be to untangle and clean them. It may be an artist who is doing this work, but it will not be work on the level of her talents. When all has been prepared, she can finally begin to embroider; at this point, it will be an artist's work.

The same is true of grace. It cannot live its life as long as it has not straightened out poor disordered nature; and it does not stop there. We call these little rectifications to which we lend ourselves, "works of grace." Yes, they are its work, but not its proper work.

In the Fifth Mansions, the Lord wishes to accept this long work and complete it. At the moment he judges to be good, he penetrates the center of the will—which has always been divided—and sets it free to love. Then, grace becomes free to live its true life, and this, let us repeat, is something new.

Jesus is come "to cast fire" (Lk 12, 49) on the earth in order to reveal and communicate divine life. His desire is that this fire take hold in our souls, not in sentiment nor in remote intention, but in reality. His sacred Humanity is the torch which can and wishes to enkindle men in the flame of the divine act. All that is necessary is that they let themselves be touched to their very center and not hold back anything of themselves from this flame. This is the grace of union, a Christian grace; it is meant to associate us with Christ.

Christ is Priest, and St. Peter looks upon Christians as participants in his priesthood (see 1 Pt 2, 5). The Council also affirms this and successively considers two aspects of the priesthood. The first corresponds strictly to the words *sacer dos:* "Giver of holy things." Through the union with God that is proper to him, Christ receives a unique delegation of the power of diffusion of self which exists in God. The members of Christ participate in this power in the measure in which they are incorporated in him: "He who abides in me . . . bears much fruit" (Jn 15, 5). The *Constitution on the Church* says the same thing when it declares that it pertains to the "laity" to cooperate in the spreading and intensifying of the Kingdom of Christ in the world.[8]

The second aspect is presenting to God the homage and sacrifice of the people. Again, the same *Constitution* wished the faithful to have some part in this act: "The laity consecrate the world itself to God."[9]

Can we think that the germ sown at baptism is sufficient to make us capable of these things? For this incorporation in Christ to become a "royal priesthood" (1 Pt 2, 9), does not Christian grace have to reach its full development—that is, genuine union with God? Can we "consecrate the world" and "give of the Holy" if we are not ourselves joined to the "holy"? It is a subject for serious reflection.

NOTES

1. v, 1:3.
2. v, 3:3, 4.
3. v, 3:7.
4. v, 1:10.
5. v, 2:1.
6. See Chap. VIII, pp. 00–00.
7. *The Way of Perfection*; cf. 20, 4–6.
8. See *Lumen Gentium*, n35.
9. *Ibid.*, n 34.

XIV
As Children of the House

The grace of the Fifth Mansions primarily establishes an attitude of will. In the ordinary way of thinking, divine union is nearly always accompanied by special joys. Teresa herself lends abundant support to this view. She underlines that they are not essential, but does not set aside this delightful aspect. In fact, she alludes to it with warm emotion when she begins to write of the Fifth Mansions.

Is it normal, then, for the objective life to bring the soul something more than the calm and serene growth which accompanies the feeling of a deep interior life? Can we speak of a "feast" of union? Why not? There is something here which causes not only a humble creature to celebrate, but all heaven as well, and the heart of God above all.

A little event from the childhood of St. Therese of the Child Jesus may help us to understand. "Mama," she said one morning, "I wish you would fondle me as you did when I was little." She had not been her usual lovable self; she had hidden from her mother's gaze and caress. Now she wanted to make up for it and, directed by a very intelligent sensitiveness, went straight to the wound in her mother's heart.[1]

Because God is a Father, he wants to find some among his children who do not play at being grown up.[2] For this reason, the total dependence of union is a feast for him. It is his Christmas. "For to us a child is born, to us a Son is given" (Is 9:6), we sing before the crib. The Divine Persons also can sing before a will which is assimilated to the eternal act: "A child is born to Us! a son is given to Us!" A child, because he is all Ours, a son, because he is like Us.

If bells ring out joyously for a baptism, announcing the divine adoption that has taken place, even though there has not yet been any psychological effect, why should not bells peal in heaven when the grace of baptism bears its fruit?

But why conjecture what the Almighty can or ought to do, when we have the testimony of the Gospel? We know for certain that the return of a sinner causes joy in heaven. Now, union of the will is nothing else than the vanquishing of sin. The sin in question is that of omission and of the abandonment of God. This sin is the source of all other sins, of that paralysis of the objective sense which is the opposite of "choosing God" and which is sin in its essence. There is no conversion nor complete repentance without this victory. But when victory is accomplished, it is the effective return of the sinner and the angels can rejoice.

Let us not hesitate to see union in this very limited light. It give us a glimpse of a new joy in the heart of God—that of the Father of the prodigal child.

We are all prodigals, however fervent we may be. We have all wasted the riches of our baptismal patrimony in a foreign land. Indeed, what is more foreign to the life of grace than the atmosphere of turning to "self" and to creatures. Now the child of God becomes conscious that he has gone astray, and begins to dream of his Father's house: "I will arise and I will go to my Father!" The Father opens his arms and his house.

This is not enough; see the feast, the dancing, the music. The whole house is filled with his joy (see Lk 15, 11–32).

St. Teresa bears witness that a soul can share here below in this feast of heaven. The Lord is sometimes pleased to introduce the soul like the prodigal, even to the banquet hall. And

there is no doubt that, like him, the soul too is astonished at
such happiness, since in the words of the Saint, it "knows not
how, nor whom it loves, nor what it desires."[3]

In what does this unknown happiness consist? Leaving aside
the parable, we can say that there is now a new psychological
situation because the will has found its true direction. By the
divine permission this well-being of the will can spill over into
the senses. Does not Teresa speak of a "delicious death,"[4] because all the faculties of the soul have been invaded?[5] This
feast brings its sign with it—the *certitude* of having been in
God.[6]

What is this mystery? Certainly not a vision, not a sight of
God. Teresa does not say that. Without going beyond the import of her words, it seems we can interpret them thus: the will
has gone beyond itself—beyond, but not into emptiness; rather,
into an efficacious realization, full of being and of life. It is a
strong act, of which it cannot help but have a sure consciousness. Now, beyond itself, there is no other fullness than that of
God. Hence, it is the power of the act to which the soul has been
invited that bears witness to its end and its principal author:
God. However little this testimony penetrates into the feelings,
this certitude is the feast of the spirit. For what else is moral
certitude than the thrill of intimate consciousness in contact
with him who *is*?

Such are the "delights" and the "riches" of the Fifth Mansions. Moreover, we must remember that these feats are an effective reverberation; that is to say, they draw the soul a little
beyond the union which would be on the plane of the will
alone.

This is quite comprehensible, for it is normal for the faculties
to tend toward being united, and for the Lord to give them the
happiness of achieving it from time to time. St. Teresa remarks
also that there is not a watertight partition between one Mansion and another.[7] And no doubt in order to encourage the soul

in its progress, it is rather necessary for it to have an idea of
what is in store for it.

Teresa presents this aspect of the Fifth Mansions very clearly
when she says that they are to the following Mansions what an
interview is to betrothal—a short meeting without commit-
ment, but still an evident advance.[8]

Nevertheless, to have a clear understanding of this stage in
relation to what will follow, we must put aside this festive
atmosphere and return to the bare idea of union of the will. It is
nothing else than entrance into pure objectivity. We have already quoted the words in which the Saint describes it under
this aspect: "True union can be attained ... by forcing ourselves to renounce our own will and by following the will of
God. If this be the case, we have already obtained union with
God. There is, then, no need to wish for that other delightful
union ... for the most valuable thing about it is that it proceeds
from this union that I am now describing. Oh! how desirable is
this union! Happy the soul that has attained to it! This is the
union I have longed for all my life and that I beg our Lord to
grant me!"[9]

Certain commentators have concluded from these texts that
there is a lower degree of union of the will. The "delightful"
union would be "mystical," the other would not. It would be a
kind of union at bargain rates for "souls of good will."

Is there not an abuse in this usage of words? If "mystical" is
synonymous with "sensible," we can only agree with their
conclusion. But what a superficial interpretation! In all that has
preceded, we have supposed that the concept of "mysticism"
represents the *reality* of the relations between God and the
soul, which are chiefly contacts with the will—contacts which
are mysterious, but positive in their effects.

St. Teresa does not say that union without "delights" is less
precious than the first. She says just the opposite. To maintain
that it is not "mystical" in the strict sense of the word would be
to reverse the order of values and to go contrary to her thought.

The simple fact of forgetting oneself sufficiently to "choose God" to the degree that implies what she calls "true union," demands a powerful interior action, and goes far beyond the capacity of good will activated by ordinary grace. The Lord produces this disposition through the leaven of spiritual delights which act on the roots of the will. This gift of the Almighty takes place on a level which is "mystical."

To think that virtuous application can supply for this divine work would be to suppose an immediate transition from the Third to the Fifth Mansions. God is certainly free to lead those he calls by other ways, but the laws of supernatural psychology remain: grace is always gratuitous, the response always free.

What we are concerned with here is really a question of emphasis. Two factors work together in raising up a soul: the attractions received from God and its own work of abnegation. One can be more conscious than the other. If God's initiative makes itself felt more keenly, the act of the will is less perceptible. If, on the contrary, the divine action wishes to remain highly secretive, the human work comes into view as if it were alone.

The distinction made by St. Teresa is certainly diminished by these differences of proportion and gradation. Therefore, we shall not speak of a "union of the will" that would not be "mystical" in the broad sense of the term; but we shall be careful to remember that this union is not necessarily "delightful." Yet, at the same time, such a nearness to God cannot occur without joy.

There is a natural joy in seeing the order of love take up its residence in us. The feast can be an austere one without it ceasing to be a feast—a family feast. "The Spirit himself," says St. Paul, "bears witness to our spirit that we are children of God" (Rom 8, 16). In lieu of "delights" he offers us this. It is the essential happiness of the Fifth Mansions. Here is his commentary: You are no longer strangers and sojourners; you are ... citizens ... and members of the household of God (Eph 2, 19).

You have the right to the kiss of friendship that he has promised to the wills he has possessed.[10]

Thus, in actual fact, union of the will, a nearness in act, appears as an intimacy. But to be more precise (for this word can suggest something a little like sentiment), it is not the intimacy of the *servant*: "No longer do I call you servants, for the servant does not know what his master is doing" (Jn 15, 15). Union is precisely a communication of the divine act.

Neither is it the intimacy of *children* who have not yet reached the age of reason, which consists in simply cuddling them. Rather, it is that of grown children, who comprehend the thoughts of their father, share his sentiments, and work with him.

Still, we must make a distinction. The older brother of the prodigal thought he was wholly devoted to his father, but he was not. He was "always with him" in caring for his goods, but he was incapable of entering into the concerns of his heart; he was at hand without being intimate.

Who can measure the distance that separates "good works" from the "work" *par excellence*, that mysterious gift of the heart which God accomplishes in union? This supreme work cannot be understood from the outside, and will always arouse some astonishment: the bad humor of the older son; the impatience of Martha. Nevertheless, it alone is expressive of the "homely" intimacy between the Lord and his child: "Abba! Father! . . . no longer strangers and aliens, but citizens of God." Consequently, it dilates the heart.

To choose God totally is much less to flee oneself than to find oneself. It is to find oneself in him—to be at home in the "home" of God, which is his life of love. It is the feast offered to all who truly wish to follow the road opened up by Teresa.

There are some who have optimistic temperaments, and this is good. Happy circumstances occur which we do well to appreciate and cultivate. There are occasions of joy in the life of faith; it is virtue to respond to them. But, let us not become confused. The joy which we have just been considering is the flower of the holy objectivity of the Fifth Mansions.

NOTES

1. See Letter of Madame Martin, Feb. 13, 1877.
2. Is not the spirit of childhood an aspect of union of the will? To hold this is not to force the doctrine of St. Therese or to depreciate that of her holy Mother. On both sides a conquest is to be made: "Unless you *become as* little children...." There is a like preparation: abnegation, tenderness, "innocence." The objective tendency has the effect of making the lover *little* before the beloved, of hollowing out a growing absence of self from the center of the heart; it is the character common to the instruction of the two Teresas, whether it be under the symbol of the Mansions or of the Little Way.
3. v, 1:3.
4. *Ibid.*
5. "Neither the imagination, the understanding, nor the memory have power to hinder the graces bestowed on it" (v, 1:5).
6. v, 1:9.
7. "In the following Mansions we shall treat of these things further and in detail, for... the experiences of this Mansion and of the next are almost identical" (v, 2:6; identical, that is, from the point of view we are using at this moment).
8. See v, 4:3.
9. v, 3:3–4, 6.
10. "Peace among men with whom he is pleased" (Lk 2, 14).

XV
Greatness and Limits

It may be of interest at this point to establish the fact that Christian perfection does not isolate itself in a world apart; rather, when some one has attained to the holy objectivity of will of which we have been treating, he has also reached a pinnacle of human values. Men have always honored energetic deeds of the will. As Victor Hugo writes:

Those who live are those who fight,
In whom resolute plan fills head and heart;
They climb the rugged mount of high career
Walking thoughtfully, in love with goal sublime. . . .

There is something important in the confrontation of the will with external obstacles even when only mediocre values are at stake, as in such purely material activities as sports. Much more ennobling are the victories which a man wins over himself. Yet these too ring hollow when they exist only on man's level, for the works which are most genuinely human are those accomplished supernaturally. The true dimension of the will is achieved in union with God, and, in raising the soul to the divine, this grace uses the energies of nature itself, it does not disdain them. Such an act transcends all human performance. Thoughtful men are conscious of this superior humanism; in our day the saints are admired less for their miracles than for their human excellence.

St. Teresa's demands in regard to the will can be harmonized with this concept of the natural side of human worth. She respects moral worth: she requires it in the service of God, she exploits its resources, overlooking its shams and deceptions.[1] But, she transports greatness to another level. When she pushes us to action, she wants to make us encounter the divine action.

Standing on this supernatural level, what greatness is brought to the Christian by union of the will? For one thing, there is a singular elevation of the virtues which St. Teresa describes as: "immense desires . . . strength to suffer . . . peace in affliction . . . detachment from all the goods of this world . . . from the dearest affections . . . discontent with this earth . . . a longing to leave this exile . . . a profound sorrow at seeing God offended . . . forgetfulness of self . . . a complete abandonment. . . ."[2] Yet these feelings are but the manifestation of a very deep vitality, the fruit of a seed which has come from above and has been completely received—the reflection of the divine act upon a will denuded of itself.

Even under this essential aspect of poverty, union is truly a sovereign greatness in accord with the law of the Gospel. Everything is promised to genuine humility, not as a reward, but by a necessary connection between this abasement and the highest supernatural realities. In the fullest sense it is the accomplishment of the Gospel maxim: "He who humbles himself will be exalted" (Lk 18, 14). Union of the will is beginning to be realized, together with all that accompanies it. We know that what accompanies it is a power of love which is guaranteed by the knowledge of how to lose oneself and to give oneself.

Then why are the Fifth Mansions only a stage? Is there something imperfect in them? St. Teresa would lead us to think so. She insists with maternal solicitude on the need for circumspection and on the risk of going backwards.[3] She says that, when we are in these Mansions, it is extremely important to avoid dangerous occasions, to implore the help of the Lord, and to examine oneself carefully, for "even in this state, the soul is not strong enough"[4] to expose itself.

True, the butterfly has pierced its cocoon. It flies, but feebly and uneasily. "It knows not where to stay."[5] The joy of union is a fleeting one; the more austere form of this grace demands a rare and painful courage.

Another disturbing aspect is also present: The "climate" of union is not an assured state, but a situation which is always being threatened. So, along with new strength, does the prayer of the Fifth Mansions also bring a certain lack of balance? More of longing than of tranquility? From what does this come? The text of the *Castle* does not tell us in precise terms, but we can gather the answer. What is under scrutiny is an act of the will. The will is not made to work alone. To have its full power and to accomplish a lasting work, it and the lower faculties must work together as a team.

Unfortunately, these faculties not only scarcely sustain it, but even pull it in the opposite direction. They are congenitally selfish and rebellious toward the objective movement. What can the pilot of a ship do if his crew is not trained, or refuses to work?

The lower faculties are not accessories in our moral life. They are an integral part of our "self." This "self" is the whole ship with its seamen; the will is only the man at the helm.

It is not enough to say the will needs to be sustained and followed. Without the concurrence of all the faculties which are associated with it in its actions, it cannot even accomplish a complete act. It can only make a rough cast of one.

The act of the will in the Fifth Mansions is a choice; it is not yet a performance. This is what St. Francis de Sales used to call a movement of the "high point," something which is very elevated and very holy, but which has neither the extent nor the stability of the perfect work.

According to St. Teresa, the act of the will is never discarded,[6] but the will must experience its limits in order to know how to find its definitive greatness in God. Thus, it will go through a progressive activity: in the beginning an obscure tendency and uncertain efforts; then an interior drama takes place; next a generous surrender which St. Teresa says grace can render full of delights when God so pleases; until finally this free orientation takes root in the whole psyche and ends in the stability of the spiritual act.

NOTES

1. "Spanish mysticism is the affirmation of the human will," says Oliveirax Martins, quoted by Jacques Chevalier in his *Histoire de la Pensée*. Paris: Flammarion, 1956, II, p. 678.
2. v, 2:6 *et seq.*
3. "Christian souls, you whom God has brought thus far, I implore you for his dear sake, not to grow careless" (v, 4:3).
4. v, 4:4, Peers.
5. v, 2:6.
6. "The whole profound Teresian dialectic supposes that we make use of our liberty *before union* and *in* union, that the soul, all passive as it is, cooperates actively in the action of God who does not act in it without it, who does not bind us without our consent" (Jacques Chevalier, *loc. cit.*).

XVI
My Heart and My Flesh

Before the will can "operate" fully, one whole part of our psychological make up needs to be "unlocked"; all those spontaneous tendencies which are summed up under the one word, "feeling." Here there is a new horizon of the spiritual life which may be disquieting. Do we have to make a place for feeling, for religious emotion, and admit this into our relations with God?

Many prudent authors point out the danger of "impressions," and the fact that the life of "feeling" is a threat to the life of the "spirit." There are trustworthy writers who glory in disregarding and disdaining this life. They believe that they possess strong spirituality because they look down on pious sentiments—which they do not have.

It is true that, for many persons, spiritual progress is linked with the mortification of the life of the emotions and affections. The pursuit of affective delights results in infantile mentalities and delusions. But do we have to generalize? Would it not be building on the unreal if we claimed to have an interior life so pure and denuded that emotions and feelings would not affect it?

The fear of "feeling" must be moderated. Such fear is necessary in many cases, especially for souls in the beginning stages. But to lay it down as a principle would be to forget that our passions are normal energies.

St. Teresa herself does not oversimplify the matter. She gives an important place to the emotions of the heart. Even the *Interior Castle*, which is meant as an impersonal treatise, is constructed in an atmosphere of warm emotion. We shall take a look with her, not into the scheme of a stylized spirituality, but into the human conditions of our development.

Christ tells us what "feeling" can and ought to be in our interior life: "When your eye is sound, your whole body is full of light. . . . If, therefore, your whole body is full of light, having no part dark, it will be wholly bright, as when a lamp with its rays gives you light" (Lk 11, 34–36).

"Your body" evidently signifies the affective powers. The context indicates this, since the body is opposed to the eye which represents the intention, that is, the higher faculties. Having admitted this, it is easy to understand our Lord's teaching. First of all, using a rather naive figure, he affirms that the instinctive psychic part of our makeup can and ought to be assimilated by purely spiritual powers which are represented by the word "light." "If your 'body' is full of light, it will be wholly bright."

There is an "if": we are warned that the result will not be obtained just through itself. And there is an assurance: if it is full of light, it will be light. In more modern terms this means that there is a perspective which normally will result in reality.

The parable goes further: once this emotional life is penetrated by the light of the spirit, it will itself be a source of light—an instrument of perfection, a wellspring of true life: "As when the lamp with its rays gives you light."

Here we have the entire vocation of our feelings. The make up of our being is in accord with this page of the Gospel. We are flesh at the same time as we are spirit, and there is nothing to be gained by avoiding what is "us" by divine disposition. We would wrong the Creator if we supposed something in our make up which would not be a means toward our goal. The flesh is one of the roads of the spirit, and it is an indispensable road for us who are not angels.

"The man who wishes to play the angel, plays the beast," was Pascal's vulgar but profound way of saying it. He meant that, not to live with all that we are, is to debase rather than to elevate ourselves.

We know well that, in our everyday life, the "heart" aids the spirit. The acts of our higher faculties are confined within this humble sphere, where they find a home to offer a kind of permanence to the interior self. Through this, they are incarnated, becoming more fully human, and in the same proportion more efficacious. There is a kind of exchange of vitality: What the body receives from the soul is returned to it in this collaboration.

Indeed, the Lord's words are verified in practice, for feeling has become intermeshed with the spirit and in its turn promotes life in depth. The soul will be able to recognize in itself this very human source of its great movements and to say with the Psalmist: "My heart and flesh sing for joy to the living God" (Ps 84, 2). How could the whole being fail to be raised up by this cry of joy?

Our divine Savior lived this law of feeling which he himself formulated. He led the affective life fully without any difficulty and with the greatest development of his higher faculties. It is the mystery of his true humanity: his heart is truly the center of himself. And when he was pleased to reveal himself in an intimate way, it was his heart which he unveiled—not his thought or his will, but his heart of flesh. This is the enlightened summit of the question—an immense horizon! A ray of beauty which transfigures "feeling" and its bonds with matter!

Not only is there realized in Jesus the perfect union of the world of feeling with that of the spirit, but through it is manifested the divine intention of consummating these two worlds in unity. Through this we again begin to see dimly that, in the divine thought, matter and spirit are not in opposition to one another; because, if they were, the Incarnation would be a paradox instead of a harmony, for between the Word and his flesh there is a concordance—a divinely willed sympathy.

Furthermore, the flesh is resplendent in him by the light of the spirit, without hindrance or violence. We are called to this same splendor; in other words, not only to the conversion of our passions and affective instincts, but to the harmony of the conscious and the unconscious, and of the things of the will and those of the emotions, in order that through this harmony our psychological unity may be realized, and in this unity, peace, so that our total efficiency is at the same time natural and supernatural.

We are far removed from this harmony, this splendor. To realize this it is sufficient to consider the scope of the Gospel challenge: "... if your whole body is full of light, having no part dark." This evidently means that no element escapes from the light of the spirit which does not tend spontaneously toward God.

What a program this is! Our powers all tending toward God? Are these the same powers which, on the natural level, only busy themselves with riveting "self" to itself, and with swelling our egotistical personality?

Luminous?—these emotions which spring from the most obscure part of ourselves? In the light of the immediate situation, those who distrust these impulses are right, and St. Teresa is among them. She knows these impulses, she points her finger at them, these reptiles of sensibility—repugnant serpents, insinuating lizards, little beasts which are not always malicious, but which manage to mix everything up.[1] All along the beautiful way marked out by the graces of God, they signal the miseries, the meanderings, the stupidities that are the products of feeling. Yet there remains the possibility of illumination, even in the lowest depths. Whence will it come? Our passage from the Gospel gives the answer: When your eye is sound, your whole body will be full of light.

Translated into Teresian language, all this—the healthy eye, the intention completely directed to God—is nothing else than union of the will. The divine light penetrating into the affective faculties is the substance of the Sixth Mansions. By her personal experience and through the observation of many souls, Teresa can affirm that this stage normally follows the preceding.

We can see how this teaching joins that of the Gospel. The symbol of the Mansions is a form of presentation proper to our Saint, but what is signified is revealed truth. The graces which constitute the Mansions and which we call "mystical," far from separating them from normal life, are really providential ways of planting good will in humanity.

The narrow bond between the Fifth and Sixth Mansions is also the best reassurance against the uneasiness prompted by the journey through the affective graces. It must be remembered that, in succeeding one another, the Mansions compenetrate each other. To pass through the Sixth means living in the austere abnegation of the Fifth, which serves as a base for all that follows. And the graces which satisfy feeling suppose and perfect the more and more objective attitude of the will.

We must never lose sight of this when reading the last chapters of the *Mansions*. The will is present there in all its vigor. God acts beyond it. But like the stone of the Holy Sepulcher, the will is the guarantee that what is done is indeed of him.

NOTE

1. "The reptiles" is an image commonly used by St. Teresa to represent the imperfect emotions of "beginners." Little by little they disengage themselves from these as they progress from one Mansion to another.

THE SIXTH MANSIONS

The characteristic of these Mansions is the divine action on the lower faculties. Here, sensibility is directly involved, and when it pleases God, intensely so. It has been thus for numerous souls, St. Teresa among them; she describes her experiences. Under her guidance, we need to discern their essential meaning.

XVII
Desert Ways

An immense program still lies ahead. It is not enough for the will to have been conquered; all the instinct must be won over by the divine Captor.

Is this impossible? No. The faculties we call "lower" are not made exclusively for common objects. They are lower in the same way that servants are inferior. The more these are motivated by high concerns, even in humble tasks, the more they are ennobled.

These faculties are inferior because they need to be perfected from outside themselves, but they are not incapable of transformation. Whether a cobweb is an accumulation of dust or a network of diamonds depends on whether it is situated in a dark corner or under the dew in the open air.

In the same way, our passions can become luminous. We have pointed it out above; we see it in the saints. When St. John of the Cross desired suffering and contempt, it was not because of a tension in his will, but out of spontaneous transport, the fresh flower of a feeling wholly seized by the Lord.

How can we come to this? We all know it can only be by an austere road. For our affections to be raised up, they must be uprooted from their first life—and every uprooting hurts; it can even be dangerous. A transplanted tree suffers for a long time. Could not God draw all the faculties to himself without submitting them to such deep disturbance?

He prefers, it seems, to lay hold of our nature in its reality, leaving it the anguish and merit of the interior battle along with the humble feeling of its limits. It is normal that every form of higher life should oppress the lower before raising it up. If God acted as a magician, the Christian would not live the drama of his life. His suffering is a sign of authentic progress—one which turns things upside down thoroughly in order to renew everything.

We deliberately speak of this sorrowful transition with a certain emphasis. Sometimes it seems that the Lord is using all his ingenuity in provoking trials, in hollowing out with his own hands the "desert ways" that his friends have to cross. Perhaps these trials are simply a surplus; we could say that suffering is inevitable here, that it results directly from the situation. This is what appears from reading the Castle.[1] Let us endeavor to untangle their two elements, exterior and interior.

The first, as St. Teresa explains, is the resistance of one's milieu. When a person has chosen to give up everything in order to seek God alone, his understanding of life no longer corresponds to that of his environment, even though it be Christian. His friends become irritated and closed to him, for they hold to their own level and do not willingly tolerate being surpassed. "A man's foes (are) those of his own household," (Mt 10, 36), says the Lord. And again: "If you were of the world, the world would love its own but . . . you are not of the world" (Jn 15, 19).

One of the consequences of entering the Fifth Mansions is a certain degree of isolation: Genuine objectivity is opposed to sin; it likewise excludes compromise. Even if the "world" had no other vice than its mediocrity, a rather painful journey through it would be necessary in order to reach the goal. St. Teresa, living very close to this world, but on an extraordinary plane, had to experience an extreme degree of this disproportion and its emotional reverberations.

St. Therese of the Child Jesus, although well protected, also experienced this clash with human judgments. Despite their wisdom, churchmen were a little winded when confronted by a child to whom the Holy Spirit had given wings. But, is it not written that, on Easter morning, John outran Peter? (see Jn 20, 4).
Even a qualified religious milieu can become terribly hostile; the history of St. John of the Cross is witness to that.

"Virtue" and "perfection," which are so readily made the subject of instructions and "edifying" conversations, sometimes coincide badly with this wholly interior reality which we call union of the will. This true life is not in the region where dialogues and encounters take place. It imposes a solitude of soul, albeit filled with anxieties.

Teresa of Avila describes at length what this exterior trial was for her. Then she comes to the second aspect of the spiritual desert, which is interior, "[The soul's] pains are indescribable," she says. "It is wrung with a nameless anguish and spiritual suffering."[2]

We may be able to comprehend something of this painful mystery by recalling what union of the will is. Perhaps then we shall understand better how to view these hidden ways in a less romantic fashion. The interior life loses nothing by being examined in a logical and intelligible way—made intelligible, that is, by someone on the outside, for such acute distress would be too disconcerting to the one who endures it for logical self-examination to be possible.

On every moral level, purely voluntary activity sooner or later produces disorder. We have seen the cause of this: the will is not made to be moved alone. We can judge by this the tension that a soul suffers when it is faithful to what we have called the "climate" of the Fifth Mansions.[3] To maintain this pure will, it has to go beyond not only its own milieu, but also its own psychic level.

This causes real imbalance, for the instincts are incapable of climbing to the height where the will wishes to establish itself. The courageous will grows anxious, for it has to maintain itself in the midst of contradiction and obsurdity.

When the Saint was describing the Fifth Mansions, she already seemed to feel the inevitable problem ahead. Remember the butterfly: from its first flight it is in trouble. St. Teresa says that, on leaving the cocoon, "it knows not where to stay."[4] So one of the effects of union is to produce anxiety. She herself warns us of it.

The conclusion must be that the objective life is necessarily a challenge as long as the Lord himself does not rally the emotions and affections. But if suffering is necessary in order to pass from the Fifth Mansions to the following ones, we do not need to invent a providential conspiracy to bring it about: the "climate" of union, that is, maintaining at any cost the gift of the will, is itself a trackless desert. Is it not all the more beautiful because of this? The suffering needed by the friends of God springs from their very fidelity. The depth of their search has earned it for them.

The Greek Fathers and spiritual writers like to give another cause for the troubles that seize the spirit in quest of the Lord. They say that God, by his transcendence, blinds the intellect and plunges it into darkness.

Theologically speaking, God does indeed keep the intellect at a distance. But here, with St. Teresa, we are searching out the paths of love, and on these paths the cause of the darkness is not in God. If God were not able to enter into contact with his creature except through darkness, the Blessed Virgin herself would have had to suffer anguish. Indeed, neither she nor any saint would have been able to be truly united to the Lord. In fact, if we supposed that God's greatness caused a vast separation, this distance could never be traversed, for it would be infinite.

Is God too great for the tranquility of our heart? A love that is

too weak may think so. Since the question is not one of understanding him, but simply of adhering to him, the Christian
mystic need not veil his face: "The Lord is near," says the
Scripture; and again: "Your face, O Lord, do I seek" (Ps 27, 8).
"O Lord, you have made us for yourself!" St. Augustine cries
out in his turn. If the Lord has made us for himself, then we are
divinely adapted for the Encounter. If something prevents such
nearness, it is not his Being, neither is it ours. What prevents it
is sin and its consequences. The story of the Fall gently
suggests this: When "they heard the sound of the Lord God
walking in the garden in the cool of the day, . . . the man and
his wife hid themselves from the face of the Lord" (Gn 3, 8).
They hid themselves because they had become sinners. But
they recognized "the sound of the Lord God," for they were
used to his visits, and it is the act of a close friend to "take a
walk" with his friends. Until then they had not felt the need of
keeping themselves at a distance.

Sin causes a shadow between God and the created spirit; it
paralyzes the latter in its proper work by the disorientation
which is the work of sin. There is a rupture between the higher
and lower faculties, since the gratuitous gifts which were in-
tended to assure unity have been lost. Indeed, why should they
remain, since "feeling" does not wish to be subordinated? It is
content in its own domain and intends to rule there; this is the
limit of its ambition.

Most of us are unconscious of such misery. Only when the
will means to live its true life does it discover its powerlessness
and isolation. Here is the great agony of the saints.

We speak of purifications, states reserved to these Mansions,
special ways that we do not have to understand. We do not
realize that this pain is at the heart of our condition. The saints
do the human race the honor of suffering from its real malady.
Everyone knows well that suffering and death are the consequences of sin. But the saints know that these are not the worst

results. In their eyes, the great punishment is not to do the good that they will (see Rom 7, 15); not to have themselves sufficiently in command when it comes to loving God, to be able to pass completely from choice to performance.

Even the choice may be imperceptible. They look for faith and love, but there seems to be no trace of their presence. What is tragically present is a tendency toward the refusal spoken of in the First Mansions, that tendency which remains in us as the mark and ferment of sin.

If this state deserves the name of "night," it is a night that profoundly illuminates the human problem. It puts a finger on the safety valve we possess, but which we are ignorant of because we do not live intensely enough.

In conclusion, perhaps we can give this violent transition a still greater meaning. Even without taking sin into account, and in the perfect unity of the faculties, there is a struggle, a risk, and a "night" when the created spirit enters into the supernatural order. To attain an unknowable goal, does he not have to choose means which to him are sacrifices and which demand a blind submission of his judgment?

Like a flash of lightning the good angels traversed this darkness. Scripture and tradition show them to us, helmeted and armed; and do not think that when a great battle in heaven is mentioned (see Rev 12, 17), Michael and his brothers fought only against the demons. Their principal victory was doubtless over themselves, that the splendor of their natures might submit to the gift of God. In this way, they entered into the divine life, marking out the way for us.

By the mercy of God we do not even have to make an act of the will in order to receive supernatural life, and we can maintain ourselves in it without too serious interior conflicts. The drama unfolds when we wish, by a genuine choice, to live it *to the full* and to persevere in this choice. Then, cost what it may, it is necessary to confront the disproportion that exists between the proposals of the Most High and our earthly being.

Nothing can exempt men from having to accept a certain estrangement from their ordinary milieu in order to arrive at supernatural realities. Our formation would cease being a summons to the summit if it did not propose a kind of obscure "ascent" to an unknown country.

In its most profound stage, this ascent is called "purification."

In short, what does being purified mean except "being delivered," psychologically speaking? Delivered from a too naive confidence in "good will"; delivered from the baseness, the fruit of sin, which blinds us; delivered from the fear of losing ourselves and of going outside ourselves.

Delivered—but at what price? We are passionately interested in ourselves, in every fiber of our sensitive life. But salvation, eternal life, says Jesus, is "to know God," and this includes total love. Our goal is to interest ourselves only in God, setting aside self-interest. And, this setting aside of self causes a distressing rending in the center of our being. But, do we know how to take the initiative? We have accomplished a great deal if we can submit to it without running away.

Through various, sometimes accidental, events, our Lord asks his friends if they are willing, not only to choose him (which they believe they have already done), but to be content with him. This is a momentous transition and follows upon the generosity of the preceding Mansions as a consequent forward movement.

How can we be surprised if there is risk, tension, if troubles occur? Is not feeling located at the juncture where spirit and flesh meet? If the burden of the spirit becomes too heavy, the flesh can faint away. The Lord cannot exempt his own from this anxiety, but once the necessary consent is given, he will deign to procure for the poor, distressed will the psychological help it needs to keep going forward. This fact, a divine gift of a new order, is what constitutes the Sixth Mansions.

However, as with the other states, we never pass completely

out of the darkness. The basic reason is that on earth, the Christian heart is always waiting: it seeks its act without being able, by itself, to do anything more than invite it and dispose itself for it. The heart's disposition is too insufficient and inadequate. Because of this, it suffers in proportion to its feelings of inadequacy, that is, in the measure in which it glimpses the goal. In this sense it is true that the night comes from the light.

"It is time for us to see each other," said the dying Teresa to her Master. Heaven alone will really put an end to our uncertain steps in desert ways.

NOTES

1. See VI, 1.
2. VI, 1:24.
3. Here and in the course of the pages that follow, we must not lose sight of the principle enunciated earlier, which is the rule of the succession of the Mansions: It is by living profoundly in the Mansions to which we have come that we are made capable of entering into the following, which takes place, however, without our abandoning the preceding (the figure of the "palmito").

   It is particularly important to note this in regard to the passage from the Fifth and Sixth Mansions, for the perfect disposition of the will is the normal condition of the divine intervention.
4. V, 2:6.

XVIII
What Shall We Do for Our Sister?

Now God is going to bring about the cooperation of the lower faculties. He is the only one who can win them over, and we can be certain that he will do so once the will's consent is given and maintained in spite of all resistance. Then the divine action is freed and becomes sovereign, although it must be positively supported by the lower faculties if it is to become stable and real.

Of which lower faculties are we speaking and how can they be taken hold of by the Lord? Perhaps we do not regard as inferior, activities which seem necessary for life and which are usually highly esteemed: the gift of working out ideas; of animating our life with stimulating and constructive images; the power of emotion. Yet, life in the spirit is above all these; it is, as we have seen, the pure life of the intellect and of the will, which are the only faculties that can communicate with God.

It is not directly possible to see, feel, or comprehend supernatural realities. Nevertheless, we know that, by the mystery of the Incarnation, God has offered himself to our exterior senses as well as to the interior ones. Therefore, their needs are understood, their rights are recognized, and Christian discipline is seen as making demands beyond self-abnegation and prudence. It proposes a very elevated use of our secondary faculties.

God himself intervenes to draw these faculties to the service of the spirit. He does so by presenting supernatural realities under aspects which they can comprehend, and by rendering these realities delightful. "God perceptible to the heart" is Pascal's way of expressing it. This must be so in order that the movement of man toward an encounter with God may become "existential." The Lord is going to mobilize the intellect and the subconscious itself in a realistic manner by a direct action that will be both illuminating and effective. St. Teresa mentions this action on nearly every page of the chapters concerning the Sixth Mansions.

Illuminating action: The soul is "never more alive to spiritual things."[1] God "discovers to it certain mysteries. He shows it some small part of the kingdom it has won."[2] It is given "a greater knowledge of the mercy and greatness of God."[3] And this knowledge is "deeply imprinted in the center of the soul,"[4] and remains "deeply engraved in its memory."[5]

Affective action: There are "delicate and subtle impulses,"[6] an ardent "feeling of love"; a "little spark flies into the soul which feels the heat"; a "delightful fervor"; a "powerful fragrance."[7]

Consequently, there is *joy:* a "storm of sweetness"; "the soul is so much absorbed in its fruition of him that this great blessing suffices it"; a "certain jubilation"; "such high favors."[8]

Joy quickens *desire:* "the soul is consumed by desire," moved by "a delicious desire of enjoying him"; "so desirous of fully enjoying him."[9]

Besides, the illuminating and affective actions are close to each other and may combine: "Sometimes, he is pleased to withdraw it from this rapture, and it at once perceives what the mansion contains."[10]

We must note especially that such joy is not had without *suffering*. The union of the two characterizes true divine action: "It is beyond the power of the devil to unite such great pain with tranquility and joy in the soul."[11]

The desire itself often causes affliction: it "consumes"; it is a "suffering which seems to pierce the very heart." It is true, however, that this pain is "all from love," and is itself desired.[12]

The Saint does not present the affective favors as producing tranquility; rather, she sees them as a succession of "trials."[13]

What are we to conclude? That the anxiety connected with the "obscure ways" is closely joined to the positive and life-giving "help" of the Almighty, and that it even grows with these new graces. This makes up the unity of the Sixth Mansions. Their function is to prepare for the perfect union with God. In St. Teresa's words: "All that serves to make her desire the Bridegroom more ardently. His Majesty, well aware of our natural weakness, fortifies her by these and other means, that she may obtain courage for a union with a Lord so great."[14]

"All that!" Now St. Teresa is including in her explanation phenomena customarily called "mystical," in the sense of an exceptionally affective intensity.

What opinion should we have concerning the divine action which accompanies the "extraordinary" graces? We must at least mention these graces as types of this action, and acknowledge in addition that they are not abnormal, since they are formally promised.

Read the Acts of the Apostles: The great miracle of Pentecost has just occurred. The crowd is gathered before the Cenacle, speechless with admiration. Peter begins to speak. Do not be surprised, he says, at what has just happened; it is what the prophet Joel foretold: "I will pour out my Spirit upon all flesh, and your sons and your daughters shall prophesy, and your young men shall see visions, and your old men shall dream dreams" (Acts 2, 17).

What do these words mean, if not that the Holy Spirit is given in order to take hold not only of free will, but of feeling as well—*upon all flesh*.[15] The Holy Spirit makes use of the things that feeling needs: inferior lights and representations, even in "extraordinary" forms.

The words, "all flesh," show that the prophet is not alluding just to the miracle of Pentecost and the analagous manifestations of the Holy Spirit in the primitive Church, but likewise to an order of things willed by God for the whole body of Christians.

St. Peter's exegesis is the first instruction given on the Holy Spirit's work among the faithful. It has the value of a doctrinal definition. It instructs us on the effects of the sacrament of Confirmation, perfecting the partial or too timid ideas we may have formed about them.

Like the whole mass of humanity, like ourselves, whoever we may be, the motley crowd pressing on the doors of the Cenacle was pulsing with emotional life. Even before they knew the requirements of the Spirit, they were given to understand that "the heart and the flesh" would have their share in his kingdom.

Hence, we no longer look upon affective graces, even when extraordinary, as improvisations of divine favor, and upon saints with "visions" as creatures of a special kind. Through the sacramental grace of Confirmation, all Christians are entitled to this kind of help, provided that they possess the dispositions which render it efficacious.[16]

Why are these gifts rare? The first answer, known well by all, is that we do not make the effort of the will presupposed by these gifts. We do not offer the Holy Spirit that "healthy eye" which does not grow weak while on the long roads of darkness and which invites the enlightenment of feeling.

But there is another reason as well. The text of Joel (which corresponds so well to the charismatic structure of the Church as taught by the Constitution *De Ecclesia*, n12) is not fulfilled in the same manner in all. Certainly the divine promise can be accomplished without being characterized by "visions" or "prophecies."

Scripture points this out to us with discernment: In the lines which conclude the Song of Solomon (and are perhaps a key to it), the brothers of the future spouse ask each other: "What shall we do for our sister on the day when she is spoken for?" The answer is: "If she is a wall, we will build upon her a battlement of silver; if she is a door, we will enclose her with boards of cedar." (Song 8:8–9).

See the tenderness of the divine plan. There are two ways of drawing a soul to the divine union: there are souls who are "walls" and they must be adorned with precious metals: there are those who are "doors," and wood suffices for them. Still it is a quality wood.

We can make practical applications by comparing our two Teresa. The great Teresa is a wall. Upon her rests the edifice of Carmel. For her, as for her companions and her other followers who would sustain the Reform, is all the richness of the "extraordinary" favors. The little Therese is a "door." Is not her doctrine a "little way"? And her only desire to make us penetrate into the sanctuary of love? Very conscious of what suits her mission, she prefers "the monotony of sacrifice" to ecstasy.[17]

This phrase deserves to be weighed, for we are acquainted with the little Saint—though poor in her choice of means, she is ambitious when it comes to the goal. She is the child who "chooses all" and who aims at "the summit of the mountain of love." Therefore, it seems that, in her judgment, "the monotony of sacrifice" can compete with "ecstasy" in preparation for perfect union. It is this that interests us, for the subject of our considerations is "genuine mysticism," not "affective mysticism."

We are not denying that the way of ecstasy is a privileged one and, on the testimony of the Saint of Avila, of a "profit so great that it cannot be exaggerated."[18] But the way of "monotonous sacrifice" has in its favor the fact that it is evangelical. And St. Teresa assures us that, "There is no need for us to receive any special gifts from God in order to arrive at conformity with his will; he has done enough in giving us his Son to teach the way."[19]

We often set limits to the evangelical perspectives. But, if we would accept the instructions of Christ earnestly, our lives would proceed along the most elevated paths, with or without special graces. Again we must note that the big question is not one of knowing whether such or such a grace will be granted us, but whether we shall take, and maintain, the necessary preliminary decisions; in a word, the essential thing is for us to be at least a "door." It is possible to be an unpretentious one, for the simple "nonchoosing of self" turns the heart into a wide open aperture. If, against all probability, others were not to profit from this, it is still reason enough to cause the will to go beyond itself and thereby merit God's doing the rest. The doves enter the dovecot through very little holes. It suffices if these holes are just their size. We make a hole of our size when we part company with ourselves.

Thus, a soul which is faithful in giving itself and in letting itself be entirely taken, penetrates by this very hidden way into what could be called the region of attraction of the Lord. It is no longer urged and impelled onward, but seized, because the interior senses are experiencing the divine lovableness; they breathe, so to speak, the fragrance of God. Then the whole being becomes capable of running toward him, drawn by his perfume (see Song 1:3–4).

All this is simple, for the Lord is not miserly with his work of drawing us to himself. Did he not say: "I will draw *all men* to myself" (Jn 12, 32). It is true that he must do so from the height of the Cross; and also that he can completely draw only those who are very near him through the total gift of themselves. But when there is this gift, it renders the graces of which we are speaking possible and authentic and normal. St. Therese is witness to the fact that these graces can act very quietly.

Let us consider these Mansions as having many nooks and corners, and that we have many ways of adapting ourselves to them.[20] St. Teresa describes the divine action as a colorful bas-relief. But this action can also take place in half-tints. Measuring ourselves against its dimensions is less important than grasping the psychological significance of the progress she pictures.

This leads us to understand, then, that as a consequence, and as a support of certain generosities on their part, some may receive imperceptible divine favors which can elevate their feelings to the level of their good will. They do not advance by very long steps; they will never fly more than a short distance; but they have their share of this Spirit who "is poured out on all flesh" (Acts 2, 17).

No matter what the surroundings, God sees the purity of the desires and of the secret choices directed toward him. The fire of heaven is ready to descend wherever it is drawn by a pure offering and a perfume of true incense.

Nevertheless, the affective elevations of the feelings are not what essentially constitute the Sixth Mansions. Rather, the fact that here God perfects the affective powers in order to make the effort of the will achieve its goal is what is essential to them. These Mansions suppose an energetic, constant and prolonged labor, and, it must be said once again, the full realization of the preceding Mansions.

Throughout the chapters we are considering, St. Teresa is careful to recall this essential point: "We must work hard and practice the virtues; that is the essential"[21]; "as it is certain that the way to please God is to keep the commandments and counsels, let us do so diligently!"[22]

NOTES

1. VI, 4:4.
2. VI, 4:5, 13.
3. VI, 6:5.
4. VI, 4:6.
5. VI, 5:13.
6. VI, 2:1.
7. VI, 2:5–6; 14.
8. VI, 4:10, Peers; VI, 6:11; VI, 7:6.
9. VI, 2:5, Peers, 14; VI, 6:1.
10. VI, 4:10.
11. VI, 2:10.
12. VI, 2:5.
13. VI, 4:1.
14. VI, 4:1.
15. "All flesh" in Biblical language signifies "our whole human being." These words express, no less truly, the human being under its affective aspect.
16. It would be in some way normal for supernatural life to make its sovereignty over nature appear. Whence comes the fittingness of the "extraordinary" graces, not for all, for that is not the order of things willed by God, but in certain cases in order to witness to the power of the grace and virtue of Christ.
17. St. Therese, Letter LXXXV to Mother Agnes, p. 128 Collected Letters of St. Therese of Lisieux, edited by the Abbe' Combes, trans. by F. H. Sheed, New York, Sheed and Ward 1949.
18. VI, 4:6 Peers.
19. V, 3:7.
20. "Each Mansion contains many more above, below and around it, with fair gardens, fountains . . ." (Epilogue).
21. VI, 6:9.
22. VI, 7:12.

XIX
Behold I Am with You

We have been looking at what the Sixth Mansions are in principle. Now let us return to the text of the *Interior Castle* to see what they are in practice. The eleven chapters which comprise the Sixth Mansions seem to address themselves to nothing but extraordinary favors, things far beyond what an ordinary soul can experience and understand.

But do not feel shut out. This flowering of the affective faculties is not the whole of St. Teresa's exposition, for it also has a meaning and a center. The center is easy to discover; through it we shall arrive at the meaning, and shall be surprised to find ourselves simply at the heart of the Christian life.

Chapter Seven particularly merits our attention. It seems placed in the midst of the others as a synthesis and a key. In it St. Teresa describes the grace of the continuous presence of our Lord. This constant presence is distinct from passing manifestations and is revealed as their source—this Jesus whom she does not see is he who often speaks to her.[1]

According to her testimony, the nearness of the Lord is the central reality here, more important and more significant in itself than the particular graces of which it is the principle. We shall see that it characterizes the present stage in a special way. In the Fifth Mansions the drama was enacted in the will; in the Sixth, the action ascends: it is the Master who takes the lead.

This may not seem a very distinctive characteristic. Is not "to be with Christ" the business of every Christian? Did he not say

to everyone on the day of his Ascension: "Lo, I am with you"
(Mt 28, 20).

Yes, he said it to all. Nevertheless, we must understand that it
is a presence he imparts at his discretion. First of all, it is a
personal matter. In whatever way we apply these words,
whether to the Eucharistic presence of the Savior or to his action in the Church, in the last analysis we must see them in
their psychological meaning, remembering that the Eucharist is
for each of the faithful—and Christians are the concrete
Church.

But not all Christians have a relationship to the Savior that
would make them capable of entering into the mystery of being
near him. Pious intentions and good sentiments are not enough
for him to be able to say "Lo, I am with you," in the full sense
required for a divine declaration. He wants to be with us; but in
order to be so in fact, we have to desire "to be with him"
through a real choice on our part. This cannot be done just by a
simple disposition of feeling. Above all, he is the Master.
Therefore, "to be with Christ," it is necessary first of all to be
his disciple—and we know the condition for this: "Anyone
who does not bear his cross and come after me cannot be my
disciple" (Lk 14, 27).

Many do try to carry their cross—some more, some less—and
thus become capable of being "with Christ." Wherever renunciation is so real that it reaches to the very center of the person,
there is the chosen ground for a living intimacy with the Lord.
This perfect form of abnegation characterizes the preceding
Mansions. In them, true disciples are formed. In the Sixth it is
natural for the soul to be "with Jesus" in the full sense of the
promise, this privileged nearness producing effects of different
order.

The Gospel gently hints that every encounter is not necessarily an efficacious one. "Who touched me?" exclaims Jesus.
"Master, multitudes surround you and press upon you" (Lk 8,
45). Nevertheless, only one poor woman had achieved real con-

tact, calling into action the miraculous power of the sacred humanity.

The mystery of these present Mansions could be expressed as the soul present to Jesus present. This is something prodigious, not only in life, but in the providential plan. The Father's intention is for us to be "with" his Son, and all his works are directed toward procuring that end. Above all, supernatural creation makes us sons of God who tend to imitate the eternal Son according to our nature, for God has "predestined us to be conformed to the image of his Son" (Rom 8, 29). The Incarnation renders man's presence to the incarnate Son possible; the Redemption unites him to the Son because of a joint obligation; and the gift of grace makes Christ present by a direct communication of the filial character.

In practice, the summit of this divine plan is found on the level of the Sixth Mansions. There, the circle of our supernatural vocation begins to close. The joining of the soul and Christ Jesus takes place as a complete psychological reality. When Jesus said to St. Teresa, "It is I," he was accomplishing his last promise: "Know that I am with you!" And, in the same action, he realized his eternal dream.

It was also the dream of the psalmist: "I will sing of loyalty and judgment; to you, O Lord, I will sing. I will give heed to the way that is blameless; when will you come to me?" (Ps 101, 1–2). In this appeal—so nostalgic and so tender—to the one who is to come, the holy singer makes evident his knowledge of his powerlessness to be himself and to lead his own life without his Lord.

He desires the "way that is blameless," that is, the way of the perfect. He beseeches the Savior to be delivered not only from punishment and from fault, but from either grave or light sin as well, because sin is a denial of being, a barrier to the fulfillment of "being." The Savior is the one who liberates the powers of the creature.

Because he is the incarnate God, close to our human psyche,

he has the right to penetrate it familiarly, to touch our emotional and affective life with fraternal ease, to work as a comrade and, as it were, by direct contact. Because this manner of working is characteristic of Christ, it characterizes the New Testament. St. Peter says so on the day of Pentecost, the threshold of a new era, in the discourse referred to above: "It is what Joel the prophet spoke of." For it is time of the visible approach of the Spirit in which, as he promised, Jesis is going to manifest himself.

Before the Incarnation, God was already asking his friends for the gift of their will: "My son, give me your heart" (Prv 23, 26). He obtained it from several, but it was hardly a matter of transforming their feelings. The Lord was leaving the gift in its pristine state, with its earthly supports and sanctions. He could not propose its full elevation then, even to his heroes, because his holy humanity is the instrument for effecting that. It will always be so. St. Teresa feels it, gives first place to the sacred humanity,[2] and declares: "The more the soul advances, the closer does this good Jesus bear it company."[3]

Our Lord himself has strong words on this point: "The Holy Spirit," he says, "will convince the world of sin ... because they do not believe in me" (Jn 16, 8–9). This is the sin of the infidels, of the atheists, of the deists. It is also the error, offensive to the Savior, of those Christians who would like to find God without Christ, of those who think, for example, that little Therese speaks too much of Jesus, that hers was the mentality of a child, while the spiritual giants have a different style.

At the risk of startling some readers, we could say that there is more spiritual greatness in lisping the name of Jesus in the context of the Sixth Mansions and on the foundations which they suppose, than in turning oneself purely toward God through harsh asceticism.

The concept of God is always inadequate, and thus, as a concept, always remains proportioned to our limitations. However loving we strive to be, our idea of God is found on the plane of reason, or at least on the plane of imagination, if not that of mere words. Christ himself securely introduces the Christian to a more theological climate, where he watches over him and makes him progress. "No one comes to the Father, but by Me" (Jn 14, 6).

This is the essence of greatness. It is acquired by practical faith in the Savior, with all that this adherence entails in the way of humble dependence. To pretend to go to God in any other way is to condemn oneself to not enjoying substantial results: It it is the poverty of non-Christian spiritualities, however venerable they may be.[4]

These sometime heroic attempts resemble the blows of the rod of Moses on the rock. The water springs up, it is true, but those who drink of it do not enter into the real Promised Land. The Lord did not say: "Strike the rock," but: "Tell the rock to yield its water" (Nm 20, 8–11). What does this mean? St. Paul informs us that the Rock is Christ (see 1 Cor 10, 4); it is not so easy to engage in conversation with him. If we want to address someone we must adapt ourselves to his language. Many would more willingly perform works of zeal and penitence than maintain, without growing weary, such a conversation with this poor and humble Master, who is so glad to speak of his cross!

"It is a great art," says the *Imitation*, "to know how to converse with Jesus, and to know how to keep Jesus!"[5] It is a great art for the Christian to become capable of the Sixth Mansions, even though through it he can be led still further.

We should realize that, at the heart of the divine presence, there is a divine operation. It is in this way that the Lord Jesus is at the center of the Sixth Mansions: "My Father is working still, and I am working" (Jn 5, 17). He works according to what he is. In him, all our affective faculties find fulfillment. Jesus is present to supply the humble needs of our humanity, our need to see, to understand, to feel. He can do so in a thousand ways from the moment in which he is "with us."

But, how does he actually do it? We have already noted that

the divine action is both illuminating and affective; it has also many other ways of appealing to the interior faculties. Sometimes these ways express an urgency. St. Teresa has a whole vocabulary in which she tries to point them out: a wound, a touch, a spark and a fire, a sweet pain which is not a pain, a hurricane of sweetness; and then the great words: rapture, flight. They can also be "delicate and subtle"—"springing from the inmost depths of the being."[6] But do not forget that, in some mysterious way, the divine call can be no less attractive and efficacious in the monotony of sacrifice, when the sacrifice is on the level of a gift of real and persevering love.[7]

It should be pointed out here that these calls come particularly from Jesus Christ.[8] In fact, when St. Teresa names the author, it is most often our Lord. And it seems from the context that, when she uses the word "god," she is thinking of her Master. Thus, she says again: "God ravishes the soul wholly into himself . . . and shows her some small part of the Kingdom he has purchased for her."[9] The preceding Mansions do not go so far. Hence, we can presume that here the Person of the Lord is always present to her, at least implicitly. Christ, then, is at work in the soul, sometimes lifting it up with sweetness, sometimes with an incomparable force, to emotions which bear his mark: exciting passions of desire, of sorrow, of generosity, and of a joy like his own.

Does he act in this way to make us feel his presence—to give us a foretaste of eternal union? Perhaps. But this is not the principal reason. His primary reason for taking such pains with our sensibility is to assimilate it definitively to his own. This should take place with every Christian. St. Paul puts it in this way: "Have this mind[10] among yourselves which is yours in Christ Jesus" (Phil 2, 5). Thus, the fruit of educating the feelings is to feel *with Christ, like Christ.*

What is the essence of this perfect life of feeling in Christ? The Apostle explains it in this way: "Though he was in the form of God, he did not deem equality with God something to be grasped, but emptied himself, taking the form of a servant" (Phil 2, 6–7). Here we have an attitude of heart, a heart full of tender welcome. And what is it that our Master Jesus so welcomes? The form of a servant. This phrase is heavy with meaning: a servant is one who has eyes only for his master; no interest but in his affairs.

In other words, the feelings of Christ are entirely devoted to the Father. He repeats it in the Gospel with a kind of passion: "I seek not my own will, but the will of him who sent me" (Jn 5, 30); "I always do what is pleasing to him" (Jn 8, 29). To have the same mind as Christ means becoming capable of going to the Father as he did—spontaneously, with his whole being. It means receiving this movement of Christ present in the deepest part of one's heart.

St. Ignatius the Martyr exclaims: "There is in me a Living Water which is eloquent and within me says 'Come to the Father!' "[11] This thought expresses the whole mystery of the Sixth Mansions. Jesus is the living water. He is in the soul as a current which carries it along. He says to it: "Come toward the Father!" because he makes it hasten with him.

The movement can be as secret as the murmur of a spring, but one which sets all the powers in motion toward their radiant Lord. It is ecstasy, conscious or not, very humble and perhaps very secret. Jesus is the author of it. In him, feeling becomes song and light. In him, it finds its ascent toward objective goodness.

NOTES

1. He who was present "was this Lord who often spoke to her. . . . Until he granted her this favor . . . she never knew

who was speaking to her, although she understood the words" (vi, 8:2, Peers.

2. "How should we wilfully endeavor to abstain from thinking of our only good, which is the sacred humanity of our Lord Jesus Christ? (vi, 7:8; and the entire Chap. Seven.)

3. vi, 8:1.

4. These few words obviously do not close the question of the possibilities of authentic supernatural relationships of non-Christians with God. There remains a vast field of implicit calls to the Savior.

5. *Imitation*, 2:8.

6. vi, 2:1.

7. The Gospel suggests to us many forms of this secret illuminating and affective action of the Lord; for example, in St. John: "They shall *all* be taught by God" (6, 45); "My sheep *hear* my voice" (10, 27); "The Holy Spirit will *teach* you all things" (14, 26).

8. See vi, beginning of Chap. Eight.

9. vi, 4:13.

10. "This mind"—that is, have in your heart the feelings of Christ.

11. *The Epistles of St. Clement of Rome and St. Ignatius of Antioch*, in vol. 1, *Ancient Christian Writers*, eds. Johannes Quastin, S.T.D., and Joseph C. Plumpe, Ph.D, trans. by Vernes A. Kleist. Westminster, Md.: Newman Bookshop, 1946; Breviary Reading for St. Ignatius, October 17.

XX

The Manifestations of the Lord

In our study of the essential content of the Sixth Mansions, we have seen that their "center" is Jesus Christ himself. Now, in trying to discover their "meaning," we cannot pass over in silence the affective forms of divine action which fill its chapters. Although to ordinary eyes these forms may appear extraordinary, St. Teresa esteemed them highly because of their effects.

It will be enough if we reflect on only one of these graces: that of visions, to throw light on them all. Several passages of the Gospel seem to indicate that such a grace is not reserved to so few that consideration of it would not be worthwhile. One passage is very clear: "yet a little while, and the world will see me no more, but you will see me, because I live and you will live" (Jn 14, 19). To this can be joined the promise which comes a little later: "He who loves me will be loved by my Father, and I will love him and *manifest* myself to him" (Jn 14, 21).

Do these promises refer simply to the appearances after the Resurrection? No; the reason given is too general, and goes beyond just the circle of the Apostles: "Because I live, and you will live"; "He who *loves* me." Christ lives for all; all his own are of the living; he is loved in all ages. It is to all of these that Jesus says: "You will see me"; and to all that he promises to "manifest himself." Still, it is a privilege, for he says at the same time: "the world will no longer see me." But, the terms

are clear. Christ announces with certainty that those who live
his life will have the happiness of seeing him.
 How shall they see him? First of all in what we could call a
vision of the Church. Is not our Creed, in its conciseness, an
"epiphany"? Does not the liturgy seek more than ever to be a
"manifestation" of Christ? The Eastern Churches find a kind of
vision of Christ in majesty in their "divine liturgies." We point
out this ecclesial aspect of the Gospel promise only in passing,
for, following St. Teresa, we purpose to consider its personal
and interior meaning. Besides, the two points of view are related: the common vision will become more real and profound
according as each of the faithful is better disposed toward the
"epiphanies" of the Lord.
 We can see that a sure, interior vision is necessary for souls
who are truly *living* in grace. A full life demands a direct,
concrete inspiration. With merely general principles and sys-
tematic applications, one can proceed "at a hen's pace," to
quote St. Teresa. Supported by hidden graces, the soul can give
much, but it cannot make use of all its psychological resources.
The proper work of the Sixth Mansions is to enable these resources to be mobilized; hence, they have to supply an enlightening experience.
 Doubtless, the "mystical" plan does not rest on the sense of
sight, as we remarked at the beginning. But, as it progresses, it
does tend to make use of sight in a certain measure: "Taste and
see," he says to us; which means: "Taste in order to arrive at
seeing" (Ps 34, 8). And again: "Be still, and know that I am God
(Ps 46, 10); the suspension of superficial activities results in
contemplative availability.
 Hence, Christ seems to show us that, even in the darkness of
this life, it is possible for men to recognize God, since he looks
for this from them. He plays an honest game and, as the condition of giving his grace, he exacts from humanity only reactions
which are properly human.

What is the chief thing that impedes our seeing? "You will see me; because I live, you will live also" (Jn 14, 19). This "because" is enough to show how rare are the souls who are capable of this life. Real living means more than being in the state of grace. It means living the life of grace itself, a life of love corresponding to the divine life from which it proceeds. We have seen that, from the beginning, this true life is called union of the will. Many do not possess it. The divine promise is for those who have merited it and persevered in it.

When Jesus says to these souls, "You will see me," what does he foretell? Would it be visions? For some, yes. But, we know that they are not granted to all who "live" the true life. Nevertheless, from the fact that they are not rare in the Church, we can deduce that the grace of corporeal vision which is granted to some may be a typical representation of the grace which properly belongs to this level of life.

Thus, in affirming "You will see me," our Lord could be understood as indicating a way of knowing him that is most often not visible in the physical sense, but is, all the same, immediate and intuitive. This puts the relationships of true Christians with their Master on a plane we seldom envisage.

Are we held back from seeing this by timidity, or by a prudent caution; or perhaps simply by the natural uneasiness of those who are used to depending on reason? People who pride themselves on sound thinking prefer to base life of the soul on principles rather than on views that seem to elude examination. The fear of subjectivism sometimes leads to a kind of rationalism. However, our Lord, who knows the rights of reason assures those who merit it: "You will see me!" Clearly he does not intend to lead his own to "illuminism." But he serenely braves positions that are too human, appealing not only to faith but to good sense as well.

Now good sense proclaims by the voice of Descartes, the father of rationalism, that the criterion of truth is after all not the reasoning, but the "evidence." When Jesus says, "You will see me!" he royally offers reason the highest of guarantees.

We are on delicate ground. Let us not go too fast, and let us recognize that evidence can be false. Some eyes confuse colors; some minds do not proceed logically; even mystical evidence is sometimes counterfeit. Nevertheless, this should not make us skeptical: correct views do exist in both the physical and moral orders. There are signs by which they can be recognized, and in which we must have confidence. The criterion of evidence retains its value; only it is necessary to state it precisely, for it is worth what the organ that sees it is worth. This will put everything into focus.

We know what good sight is in the spiritual domain. The Gospel teaches in clear terms: "When your eye is sound, your whole body is full of light" (Lk 11, 34). It is a question of the integrity of the will. The healthy organ, then, is the will that is perfectly objective. The preceding Mansions bring this out. Although the guarantee of this is supernatural, it also contains a very reassuring natural element: supreme impartiality.

Once again, we are verifying the necessary relationship between the Mansions and the fact that those we are now studying can be prudently considered only on the basis of the preceding ones.

"You will see me *because* you shall live." Indeed, if the Lord offers an intuition of himself, it will surely be received if we are on the plane of true life—which is true love.

There are many ways Scripture expresses the fact that a secure enlightment springs from obscure but total adherence to Christ: "He who follows me will not walk in darkness but will have the light of life" (Jn 8, 12); "He who does what is true comes to the light" (Jn 3, 21). Perhaps, there is still narrower connection between true life and true light, for after having said that the Word is life, St. John adds: "That life was the light of men" (Jn 1, 4).

Thus, the genuine life that makes us live not only leads to the

light, but is one with it. It cannot live hidden. The gifts of the
Sixth Mansions, considered in their essence, properly speaking
are not gratuitous, for once true union is granted, they are in
some way inevitable, just as the dawn cannot not give light
when the sun is on the horizon. Such is the profound connection supposed by the promise of the Savior: "You will see me
because you shall live." These words are most reasonable because they offer the criterion of evidence only to an organ
which is perfectly "in focus."

But, practically speaking, what is this light that is linked to
love, identical with life, and offered to all? Before naming it, we
can conclude from what preceeds that it is not only an intuition, but a definite revelation—something which comes from
life and stirs the powers of life. Jesus offers it to his own and not
to the world, because the world is not capable of it: "The world
will see me no more" (Jn 14, 19).

To him who wishes to see the Lord and to him who wishes to
love him, we apply the words of St. Paul: "He did not count
equality with God something to be grasped, but emptied himself taking the form of a servant" (Phil 2, 6–7). To know how to
empty oneself in order to become totally receptive ("entirely
teachable," as Sister Elizabeth of the Trinity used to say[1]), this
is the way of knowledge according "to the spirit." Now we can
understand the vision promised us: a definite rapport with God
in complete dependence, a contact which is a flash of light. St.
Thomas calls this contact by its name: faith.[2]

The mass of Christians take faith to be the adherence to truth
through the intermediary of formulas: opaque formulas which
yield obscure faith. When the act of faith is thus understood, no
matter how great it may be, it leaves the mind outside of what it
believes, on the level of mere formulas. The defined formula
brings a certitude that is primarily negative; it is a wall that
marks off the limits of religious thoughts; it follows the proper
meaning of the word "definition."

The whole of faith is not there. The faith of the patriarchs, the faith of the holy Virgin, is something else. Indeed, we may speak of living faith but not know what it is. We may see it as the beginning of the interior life for the generality of Christians, while in reality it is found at the summit of the graces of vision in the Sixth Mansions.

St. Teresa establishes a hierarchy in these graces. Corporeal visions are at the lowest degree, then come imaginary ones, and finally the intellectual.[3] The dignity of the grace is in inverse ratio to its affective content. The criterion for the greater dignity is the greater quality of certitude and the more intimate penetration of the object known.

In this world, the most intimate penetration and the most positive certitude are found in true faith. What it attains to cannot be limited to the sum total of the ideas our mind is capable of forming; and, for this reason, it ushers us into the obscure. But it sees, in a sense which is proper to the Evangelist St. John. For him, the ideas of sight and of light relate essentially to the perfecting which procures for our being contact with the Being. Is this not really to see truth in its source? It matters little that this truth is not clothed in sensible or intellectual forms, for these would put it on the level on which we see according to common standards. It is vision because it is perceived by the intellect directly, received in a way sufficient to be communicated to the will and to give information to the life. All graces of "vision" only tend to raise the soul to this essential vision. And yet, it is of faith because of the submission that it demands, the submission of love that was already required in the preceding Mansions and which here attains an altogether new depth.

For this reason, this solid, living faith, the fruit of the Sixth Mansions, bears more resemblance to the vision of heaven than the graces of vision which are supposedly gratuitous, for there is nothing accidental or gratuitous in the vision of heaven. It springs directly from the potential of charity in the soul. The same is true of perfect faith. Hence, it deserves to be promised by the Lord in a higher degree than the most beautiful apparitions. And his words do not deceive.

"You will see me." True faith is not just darkness. Even here below it must become light in the way that Christ Jesus already proposes to us, by being assimiliated to the Truth that is himself. We are called to "see" in the "light of life" him who enlightens every man who comes into the world (see Jn 1, 9).

St. Paul also speaks many times of this assimilation and tells us its manner: "Put on the Lord Jesus Christ" (Rom 13, 14), he advises in the Epistle to the Romans. And, to the Colossians, he says: "Your life is hid ... with Christ in God" (Col 3:3). Is that not the mystery of the living contact which is the foundation of the whole Christian life?

The Letter to the Ephesians tells us how this contact is light at the same time that it is life: "May Christ dwell in your hearts through faith ... that you may have power to *comprehend* with all the saints, what is the breadth and length and height and depth of Christ's love, and to know the love of Christ which surpasses knowledge that you may be filled with all the fulness of God" (Eph 3, 17–19).

All of St. Paul's words are meaningful. The text presents to us, in an abridged way, living faith, the dwelling of Christ in the heart, the source of an understanding of immense perspective, in the measure of Christ himself, penetrating even to that supreme depth of Christ which defies every other mode of investigation—his love.

St. Paul notes that this education in love is an indispensable prelude. In the first place, he says, "May he grant you to be strengthened in the inner man" (Eph. 3 , 16). He also declares briefly to what the "vision" of faith tends: the fullness of the soul in God. This sums up in a few lines the last three Mansions of the *Castle*. This spiritual road was known by many in the first days of Christianity. Christians capable of living the Sixth

Mansions must have existed then, for their entrance into the Church demanded generosities which put them immediately on the level of renunciation required by these Mansions.

Should not the same profound gift of self obtain the same sight of Jesus in every age? St. Therese of the Child Jesus used to say that she lived "in the light which fell from the closed eyes of the holy Face." This was not a perceptible vision; nor was it one of words. How many souls shine in the Church simply because, their eye of faith being open, they are living reflections!

NOTES

1. Prayer of Sister Elisabeth of the Trinity which can be found in The Praise of Glory: Reminiscences published by the Carmel of Dijon trans. by the Benedictines of Stanbrook Abbey (Burns, Oates and Washburn, 1912), or in the commentary by Dom Eugéne Vandeur, O.S.B., Trinity Whom I Adore (Pustet, 1953), New York & Cincinnati [trans. from French by Dominican nuns, Corpus Christi monastery Menlo Park, California].

2. He says that the passion gets its efficacy through a spiritual contact, that is to say by faith and the sacraments of faith (Summa theologica Q. 48, R. 6, ad. 2)

3. For the different kinds of "visions" see Fr. M. Eugène's very detailed study in I Am A Daughter of the Church. Père Labaud, in his profound Life of Nicholas of Flue, sums up on this point the doctrine of the Fathers, that of Blessed Henry Suso, and that of the saints of Carmel.

   From a note in the Autobiography of Saint Teresa, edited by the Carmelites of Paris, is taken the following résumé: The corporeal vision takes place through the eyes of the body;

the imaginary vision takes place by means of the imagination. It is through a divine operation on the imagination, not
by a representation destitute of reality; the intellectual vision takes place through the intuition of the intellect. Father
M. Eugène distinguishes among these last, visions of substance having a body (e.g., the presence of our Lord Jesus
Christ) and the perceptions of objects which are purely
spiritual.

XXI
The Gift of Freedom

The divine action makes itself dominant at this stage of spiritual progress. Is there any limit to Christ's power of taking possession of the whole soul? Teresa is not afraid to say no; it is in some way irresistible. When her desire for heaven has become a torment, she asks: "Would the soul not be able to resist acquiescing in the will of God which holds her here on earth?"—"No," she answers, "she can no longer do so."[1] But then, what about liberty, merit. the human value of life where such souls as hers are concerned? Does spiritual progress necessarily challenge the moral aspect of perfection? This includes the problem of "passivity" of which mystics speak: Does "to be passive" mean ceasing to be active or autonomous or oneself?

The concept of freedom that we may have acquired at school is apt to be of little use here, for it is usually based on experimental ideas which scarcely go beyond pointing out possible illusions and limits; when asked for a definition we are forced to an avowal of helplessness. Should not something so closely connected with our human problem be looked at from a higher point of view? The wise and holy St. Thomas offers us the insight of a less hesitant psychology based on the divine idea of human nature.

We learn from him that two elements concur in an act which is truly free: a firm choice of the end, and the possibility of choosing the means.[2] The first element, the principal one, makes freedom an interior power. The second is easy to understand and is important, but it does not suffice in itself to constitute freedom. If freedom were only the ability to choose, all its greatness would be in its autonomy, and the possibility of a bad choice would be a part of this greatness. To understand liberty in this way would be to characterize it by its weakness, as if we defined life as the possibility of dying, or royalty as the possibility of abdicating. If "to be free" means choosing the more difficult act, this might raise it above ordinary decisions and permit one to claim a certain nobility, but such a "liberation" would be only on the level of the means.

True freedom can be compared to the needle of a compass. The autonomy of the needle is the result of its being very mobile on its pivot; its power is its magnetization. If it were only mobile, it would simply be inert, at the mercy of the impulses of shocks and air currents. If it were magnetized, but fastened or caught, its magnetization would be of no use to it.

It is the same with us: moral freedom is an interior exigency in a fixed direction with a radical possibility of following it. We are free in the measure in which we are more strongly magnetized and more freed from foreign impulses.

Man's heart needs help from this double point of view. What else are the graces of the Sixth Mansions than a setting in order of freedom: God's capture of the emotions a magnetization, trials a means of liberation directed to breaking our bonds. In one way or another, the Lord touches feeling in order to incline the will toward its choice; our nature will have it so.

St Augustine compares this action of the Lord to that of a shepherd offering a green branch to the sheep: he concludes that both attraction and pleasure are legitimate ways of allurement when they come from God. Such action on his part involves no trifling with free decision, no pilfering of anything from personal choice, for here the divine action is working in view of a choice already made: the heart has said its great "yes" in the preceding Mansion. Now the soul's progress consists in being raised above itself in its own consciousness; it is so strongly magnetized that the power of its interior orientation defies every inclination of lesser value.

We must look upon free choice from this viewpoint. The rosebud does not open all by itself. It needs a ray of sunlight to make it unfold. But it tends to that effect and the ray does it no violence. Would the honor of the rosebush require that it be planted only in the shade? In this same manner, God, who has raised up and sustained our good will, makes it achieve its end: God "prospered him in his labors and increased the fruit of his works" (Wis 10, 10). If this work is ours at the moment when grace incites it, why should it be no longer ours when grace transforms it?

Seen in this light, the moral path is broadened. Without forgetting our limits, we can extend our horizon. We remain ourselves beyond ourselves: God wants us to be immense in him.

Without doubt it is the divine action that makes us capable of this. But because the created will has previously chosen to love, it can now call its own the power of love which is given to it. And if this power draws it and surpasses it, it can still say that this consequence is its own and is one with its love.[3] There is no reason to fear competition between the sovereign attraction of grace on our affective faculties and our moral responsibility. One does not supplant the other, each needs the other.

St. Therese of the Child Jesus may seem to think otherwise when she expresses the wish that her free will be taken from her in order that she may depend more on the divine action.[4] It is her way of aspiring to complete freedom. Conscious of having made a right election, she wants her act to be eternal; she is asking for the freedom of heaven.

It is precisely this total freedom that attracts one who has come to love "with all his soul." St. Paul glories in it: "It is no longer I who live, but Christ who lives in me" (Gal 2, 20). A substitution of responsibilities? Not at all; rather, the height of freedom.

The value of a decision does not depend on long deliberation, although this may be necessary when one does not see clearly. The light of the Holy Spirit can make a clear and unhesitating decision immediately possible. We hear the Blessed Virgin asking a question before saying her "fiat"—she does not ask for time for reflection.

The divine perfecting granted to the heart in order to speed it toward its goal, also enlightens it in regard to immediate choices; as St. Thomas says: "In Virtue of its impetus toward the end, the will turns itself toward the means; what it desires in these is the end."[5]

Here the Lord is again taking the initiative as Creator. What a difference from the preceding stage where everything seemed to hang on a human "yes"! St. Teresa affirms that now the Lord does not even ask for consent; he is completely the master. Why was he not that before? Because it was the little creature's turn to play its part. Henceforth he will lead the way; all that is firm realization, all that achieves its purpose, is his work.

In creating the material world, he was not content simply to produce elements, he also organized them. In the spiritual order, would it be worthy of him to abandon the raw material of salvation to our blundering actions? According to the Epistle to the Hebrews, he is the "Author and the Finisher" (Heb 12, 2 Douai), and St. Paul can well write the Philippians: "I am sure . . . that he who began a good work in you will bring it to completion" (Phil 1, 6).

How? Let us turn to Genesis: we notice how quiet are the divine interventions in making the world. The word "create" is scarcely used except for the first act. Afterwards come unpretentious terms: God "made" the firmament; he "set" there two luminaries; he "gives orders" to the waters, to the earth. . . . Different modes of action that could be called elaboration, or even collaboration . . . sovereign power guides the universe by directing its existing energies.

In like manner his spiritual action penetrates into the very heart of the instinctive powers, utilizing them without coercing them; it eliminates nothing that belongs to them, but sets them in motion on a higher level and thereby looses freedom from its bonds.

This work, which is organized and completed from above and from within, can well be called one of discrimination. In the beginning God *separates* the light from the darkness, he *divides* the waters from the waters, he *distinguishes* the day from the night. . . .

The New Testament describes the same action in the world of souls: "God's word is living and active, sharper than any two-edged sword, piercing to the *division* of soul and spirit . . . and discerning the thoughts and intentions of the heart" (Heb 4, 12).

There is great need of this, for the conflict between instincts and the will causes much confusion. Even when the will manages to emerge, light is lacking, because, mingled with the darkness of the "flesh," it is not really light. A sovereign hand is needed to penetrate even to the "joints and marrow," to take hold of the light, hand to hand with the darkness "to the division of the soul and the spirit." Then the waters of heaven are gathered together and everything becomes "living and effectual."

The saints experience this. Listen to St. Teresa, freed one day from attachments that had paralyzed her: "I did not think that I could ever give them up . . . I had tried it already, but I had put the idea aside . . . Then the Lord set me free and gave me strength."[6] She was conscious that everything that was best in her, after all her own seeking of it, was hers at last from God.

He, respectful of existing values, had discerned the earnest will immersed in elusive obstacles. He had put the interior psychical chaos into order, and strengthened the powers of life. St. Teresa sums up this divine activity as the gift of freedom.[7]

This is an expressive designation; it is a freedom that is given; the more the will is "magnetized" by God, the freer it becomes. To be touched by him in the center of one's being is not submission to a foreign influence; rather, it means receiving a complement of being. God wishes us to be "us" more that we can wish it for ourselves. He handles his creature as its Master, only the better to achieve and guarantee its proper form (cf. Ps 100, 3).

His gifts can anticipate our choice, but for all that they do not replace it. The act of election is always ours, although its immediate aim may be given us. It is not indispensable for the will to realize this, it is enough that it accepts it.

"Mama," said a little girl, "I am happy that you are my mother. If God had made me choose among all mothers, I would have chosen you." She had found the way to make an election, where ordinarily the heart follows its natural bent without making a choice.

It is the same with the soul and God. Under the sovereignty of him for whom she is made, she remains free to choose him. The more the Lord possesses the soul, the more it clings to him in full consciousness of its own interest and disposition. The essence of spiritual freedom is to act through knowledge and love.

There is a great deal of talk today about "depth psychology" and of how to regulate our automatic reflexes. Would not the surest way be that of the saints as set forth by St. Teresa? It is wholly contained in the passage from the Fifth to the Sixth Mansions: to use our voluntary control to the utmost, however limited its domain (aided, of course, by grace), and through this, to obtain that God will take care of the rest. . . .

Indeed he claims this share of the action (as we see in Osee 14, 6–8); it is like the dew which refreshes and vitalizes. Then, says the prophet, the lily rises straight toward the heavens, the trees take root and multiply and receive beauty and fragrance . . . it is also like the shade, the place of rest which protects the seed.

Shadow and dew—the double aspect of the encounter of our psychic nature with its Creator. Under the sign of dew, freedom asserts itself and the spiritual act matures, no longer a fragile shoot, but a ripe fruit bathed with the sun. And yet, says the Scripture, in the shadow . . . for it is a mystery, the very mystery of the encounter. It is right to look upon this fruit which is received from God as his, without its ceasing to be ours. This is the conclusion of the prophetic text and the deep meaning of the act that is fully free.

NOTES

*The text of this Chapter XXI is that of Chapter XXIV, "Le don de la liberté" from *Aux Sources de l'Esprit,* by Madeleine de St. Joseph, Maison Mame 1974; it replaces Chapter XXIII "Créateur et créature" of *En Esprit et en Vérité* by the same author. The substitution is made at her express request.

1. VI, 11:5.
2. Ia IIae 12, 4.
3. "My love is my burden," St. Augustine.
4. *The Story of a Soul,* p. 276.
5. Ia IIae 8, 2.
6. *Life,* of St Teresa of Jesus.
7. The "grace of Christmas" in the life of St. Therese has an identical meaning and produces the same effects. On that night she "began to run as a giant."

XXII

As the Gentle Breeze

The Sixth Mansions imply an elevation of the sensible faculties. Although this promotion corresponds to our nature, and may be willed by God, we may ask how far it can go. Does this in some measure diminish the "spiritual" character of charity? We may have the impression that the pure movement of the will is more noble; an incomplete reading of St. John of the Cross may tend to make us disdain "affective" graces. So a clarification may be useful.

God deigned to pass by Elijah on Mount Horeb. But he did not pass by in pure "spirituality"; a light breeze preceded him as the sign of his presence, a sign also, perhaps, of a divine intention: body and soul are made to vibrate together. But not by just any kind of vibration, for the sacred text informs us: "A great and strong wind rent the mountains and broke in pieces the rocks before the Lord—but the Lord was not in the wind; and after the wind an earthquake—but the Lord was not in the earthquake; and after the earthquake a fire—but the Lord was not in the fire; and after the fire a small still voice. When Elijah heard this, he hid his face in his mantle and went out and stood at the entrance of the cave. There came a voice to him . . ." (1 Kgs 19, 11–13). It was the Lord.

Notice the always more "spiritual" manner of the phenomena that announce the coming of God: the furious wind that rends the mountains, the earthquake, the thunder and lightening, and finally the small still voice.

We can conclude that, if feeling is to be associated with the spirit, it must be proportioned to the spirit: that is, subject to the life of the spirit and disposed to submit to its rhythm. The Lord is in the "gentle breeze" because it is gentle.

Picture the sea on a calm day. The swell that ruffles its surface is not an accidental agitation. It does not come from the land or the air; they say it is caused by the stars. So it must be with the movements of purified feeling; they come from on high. They are indeed movements of the emotions and affections, but they are ruled and measured by the sovereign rhythm of the "spirit."

At the end of the Sixth Mansions, where Christ is at work, the result of the divine action is this harmony between flesh and spirit. Is not this one of the most important effects of the mystery of the Incarnation? Is it not exactly the one concerning which the Church sings in the Preface for Christmas: God seen by men that we may be drawn by him to the love of things unseen?[1]

When we analyze the deep meaning of this text, we see two degrees in the revelation announced by the divine Child: one sensible; the other more elevated and suggesting a direct intercourse with the invisible world. This latter degree is the supreme vocation of the heart. To know God under the form that makes him like to us is the beginning, the education of the sensible through the sensible. The goal of this education is the immediate affinity between the sensible and the spiritual reality.

This mystery of assimilation seems to confuse the two elements of our nature and their proper objects. This mystery must be accepted. In a way known only to God, it achieves the unity of our being.

The words of our Christmas liturgy sum up in a marvelously concise way the work that is accomplished psychologically by the "God who is with us." They teach us the real meaning of "rapture," whatever its form: "We are *drawn* by him," sings the Church. It is a lifting up of the heart, a transporting of the sensible beyond its natural limits; it is the fruit of the Sixth Mansions.

The purpose of these sensible movements is not to exalt feeling in itself, but to detach it from its own milieu in order to attach it to the milieu of the spirit.

We should not think that this deepening is accomplished in a growing intensity of emotion. Rather, it takes place in a growing refinement of perception. Nor does it mean that feeling has to comprehend to the fullest extent possible the tangible aspects of supernatural realities; rather, it need only reach a kind of direct relationship with these realities.

The Blessed Virgin knew this growth in the "feeling" of divine things. She had the experience of face-to-face communications with her divine Son; and her heart penetrated these exchanges immediately so that she could live them in their entirety. After the Ascension, there were no more exterior communications, but this did not mean they were absent, nor was Mary's sensibility weakened. The Holy Spirit came upon her as he did upon the Apostles, in order to vitalize everything. In this world, she already enjoyed the perfection of the life of the heart.

Hers was an ever-ascending perfection: she was not at the peak of her earthly life at the time when she cradled and nursed the Word made flesh; nor at the hour on Calvary when she lived his death. For the holy Virgin, as for her children, the law was always to go from the lesser to the greater. Thus, during the years that preceded the Assumption, she lived an indescribable progress; and her death, hidden in silence, was the final consecration of the ascent of her heart to the invisible, and of the refining of her love.

By drawing near to God in this manner, although in a measure which is beyond our imagination, Mary approximates the state of the first Christians, her children. Although she is unique in her visible participation in the mystery of Jesus, yet, in what concerns adhering to him in spirit, she opens up a way that is valid for *all*.

How can we visualize this going from the sensible to the spiritual? Is there a place in our psychology for what certain thinkers call the "sensation of the divine"? Will God ever be found on the level of sensation? No; only in ourselves are the sensible and spiritual called upon to unite. But how can they accomplish this?

St. Thomas has a thought that may help us get some notion: "The soul," he says, "must love in charity, charity itself."[2] In its immediate meaning, this statement alludes to a *spiritual* love of the good, which is charity. But is there any reason why this spiritual disposition may not be sustained by a delicate *taste* of the charity that should be the flower of feeling, that has been cultivated by the divine action?

We see in Christ Jesus this perfect and delightful repose of the sensible in the spiritual act: "My food is to do the will of him who sent me" (Jn 4, 34), he says. The idea of food includes that of a sensible satiety. We should realize that this tendency toward the Father, which is the whole will of our Lord, procures for his lower faculties all the delights that they can desire. They are not capable (and ours still less so) of being fed immediately by God. Their share is to rejoice in the fullness of the spirit's satisfaction; their function is to be, as it were, greedy for it, crave it, and for this reason to intervene without ceasing in the objective life of the spirit—no longer to weigh it down, but to stimulate it. The "sensation of the divine" cannot be a direct contact, but only the sensible echo of a spiritual encounter.

It is important to remember this, for sometimes very earnest souls are led to forget that "God is spirit and those who worship him must worship him in spirit" (Jn 4, 24).

Two worlds exist in us and they are destined to be united, but only in subordination. The glory of the inferior world is to attain to serving the other. But, in spite of this fact, it will never penetrate into the real life of the spirit. Normally, even the cooperation of the affective faculties will sometimes seem to be kept at a distance by very high spiritual operations. St. Teresa notes this in the last chapters of the *Castle*, in relation to the Sixth Mansions.

The high peak of desire for God is not a culminating point of feeling; it lies beyond feeling. *All* takes place, says St. Teresa, "in the very depth and center of the soul, where this thunderbolt reduces all the earthly part of our nature to powder. At the time, we cannot even remember our own existence."[3]

Who knows whether the terrible agonies described by the Saint are not the last attempt of the "sensible" trying to go beyond its own domain because of its craving for a "sensation of the divine"? The "divine" reserves itself for the spirit, and the heart still does not know how to accept its own limitations.

We should note that this transition can be realized only at the price of a truly dramatic struggle. Just as earlier the decision of the will clashed with the resistance of the feelings, so also here there is a conflict between sensibility won over to God and the privileges of the spirit.

Conquered by the divine approaches, sensibility becomes exacting and aspires to taste and feel God in himself. But this is an impossibility as we have seen. According to St. Teresa this ardent desire and its inexorable limitations mark the last act of the Sixth Mansions. She calls it a pain of great price which bears final witness to the high elevation of feeling. But feeling must be brought back to its secondary role. Therefore, covetousness must be humbled; it is accomplished to the maximum degree by the fruitless intensity of its own burst of endeavor, which breaks it to pieces. It is the supreme "purification."[4] Feeling, overflowing and raised up, has been able to exalt itself; now, at the peak of its ascension, comes its amendment.

At the same time, an ambiguity is cleared up: the meaning of "possession" in regard to divine realities. To possess God is the dream of the interior man, but who really knows what it is? He desires to possess God like a treasure that he receives into himself, that he takes hold of, and by which he is enriched. But God does not give himself in this way. As long as the soul does not go beyond this idea, it is not fit to possess him.

The Lord alone has the right to possess his creature. He gives himself by making himself master of all his creature's desires, leaving it only the craving of being possessed. This fills its spiritual need to the brim, for, as we have already remarked, the spirit's life is to lose itself in the life of God. *That* is the possession of God, for the soul, laid siege to by God, is assimilated to his life.[5] When it is wholly in this disposition, it has endured the last trial.

From anguish it comes to peace; the affective life has become a gentle breath, both exteriorly and interiorly. St. Teresa points out that its rarefaction reaches such a degree that the soul is no longer conscious of its own existence. The strong vibrations are growing weaker; peace descends.

Peace is a feeling—so near to a spiritual perception that it may be said to have no mass. It does not seek itself; it loses itself in the movement of the spirit, and is ceaselessly reborn in it, for it is the nature of supernatural vitality to give life in God to whoever denies himself for God. Thus, the most delicate of feelings is maintained in the existence proper to it, for the Lord is not willing to disincarnate the human spirit. This feeling, however, like all others, lives by a total submission to the Spirit.

Peace characterizes the Seventh Mansions. Therefore, peace is the sign that the preceding ones have done their work and that transition is taking place. It seems that nothing can more clearly or more decisively differentiate this last stage from what

has preceded than the definitively established precedence of
the "spirit" over feeling.

NOTES

1. "By the mystery of the Word made flesh, the light of your
   glory has shone anew upon the eyes of our mind: so that
   while we acknowledge him as God seen by man, we may be
   drawn by him to the love of things unseen" (Preface for
   Christmas).
2. *Summa* II^a–II^{ae}, q.25, a.2.
3. VI, 11:2.
4. "Her pains purify her soul, so that it may reach the Seventh
   Mansion, as Purgatory cleanses spirits which are to enter
   heaven" (VI, 11:6).
5. To tell the truth, St. Teresa is without misgivings at the idea
   of "possessing God." Thus, in VI, 4:14, she remarks about
   the joy "of possessing for our own ... the Lord of all treasures." We think, nevertheless, that the present reflections
   correspond to the meaning of her doctrine.

THE SEVENTH
MANSIONS

This is the culmination of the preceding states, the state of equilibrium, in which the fruits of the Spirit surface. But it is not a *heavenlike* state: suffering has its place here; faults are still possible; humble virtues are its sign. Nevertheless, union with God is as perfect as it can be in this life. For interior unity has been realized, and the whole being concurs in the life of charity.

XXIII
A Heart that Loves You

It is almost classical to picture the Seventh Mansions as a kind of glorified ideal. Yet we are not pretentious in scrutinizing them, for if they are a summit, it is not a summit lost in the clouds but one that is no higher than our vocation as Christians. However insignificant we may be, may we not gaze on the heights of heaven? And may not the humblest of travelers try to see, even if only from afar, the home that awaits him?

The first aspect of this final stage is wholly one of simplicity: order and peace reign in the soul. There are no whims, no contradiction, for the world of sense and feeling is subordinated.

How can we get an idea of this new life, which is a new manner of loving? It must be the peaceful triumph of objectivity. "I am ascending to my Father" (Jn 20, 17), says Jesus; "Father, I am coming to you" (John 17, 11). The Lord has conquered a soul and brought it into conformity with his own. The desire of the Apostle is then realized to the full: "Let this mind be in you which was in Christ Jesus" (see Phil 2, 5). It is the love of a child who goes on his way without swerving.

St. Teresa shows us how to translate this into practice when she says that the first effect of the new life is "a self-forgetfulness so complete, that [the soul] really appears not to exist... it seems entirely occupied in seeking God's interest[1] ... it seems no longer to exist."[2]

Listen to our more contemporary St. Therese sounding the same note: "It is impossible, I know, but if God were not to see my good actions, I would not be the least bit disturbed by it. I love him so much that I should like to please him without his being aware of it. When he knows it and sees it, he is obliged to reward me and I don't want him to have to go to this trouble."[3] And again: "O my God, even if my suffering was really unknown to you, I would still be happy to have it."[4]

What a difference this is from the preceding Mansions, especially that eleventh chapter where everything was aspiration! There the heart wanted to "possess" its God, but had not yet learned that, since God is Love itself, when he gives perfect charity he gives himself.

After our long ascent, when we think we are coming out on a lush plateau to sit down to the "feast of love,"[5] must we renounce the reward and cast aside the delights of communication? We need to understand the matter better: the real reward of objectivity sought is objectivity found—the candor, the simplicity of a love that is no longer anything but love. This is better than any communication, for this is essential assimilation.

Indeed, the two Teresas are not being reactionary when they speak as they have just done. Their indifference is spontaneous and full of happiness. St. Paul himself explains it: When charity lives in a soul in its fullness, it is because it "has been poured into our hearts through the Holy Spirit" (Rom 5, 5). When we possess this divine Spirit and act in him, have we not already received his reward? Furthermore, we are learning love in itself and drinking it at its source. But love coming from this divine source is not what we may know as love, that is, an exchange of feeling in which we give with one hand in order to receive with the other. God does not enrich himself in loving us any more than he does in loving himself. He takes possession of himself by way of knowledge not by way of love.

The Father loves the Son, the Son loves the Father; yet, this love does not have two starting points, since it is a doctrine of faith that the Holy Spirit proceeds from the Father and from the Son as a single Principle. Thus, properly speaking, it is not an encounter and a bartering in love.

In his Trinitarian love, God gives himself and does not receive himself. He is satisfied in the very act of love. And when he draws near to a soul in an intimate way, he overwhelms it with this happiness; he makes it an act of love like himself. A soul which has been lifted up, attracted by the divine, has scarcely disappeared from sight in fixing itself upon its Lord, when this very Lord comes to meet it. The path is short from love to love. The soul has been accustomed to advance through a movement of offering; but now this movement is spared it. The gift of itself is given to the soul in the gift of God that comes to it.

Certainly this is something divine, and yet profoundly human also. St. Teresa feels this. She remarks that, before God admits a soul to the spiritual marriage, he introduces it to the Seventh Mansions, that is, into the soul's center which is his dwelling place. By this she seems to suggest that such a high union with and resemblance to God have their roots in the mystery of our being.

This is so true: even in this we are images of God. And it is also true that the deepest need of our heart is to desire God above ourself. But this marvel, this innate instinct which lays hold of and transforms the grace of Baptism—only the progress of charity can let it be discovered.

Sin and its consequences keep us on the surface of ourselves![6] The majority of men do not know themselves, even those who have done their best to reflect upon themselves.

The divine light must invade everything before it can shed its ray into the real center of "self." When that happens, there is, along with other things, a changed way of looking at the mystery of the person. It becomes clear that the center of gravity in a human being is not in himself but in God.

"Seek yourself *in me*," were our Lord's words to St. Teresa; and she had merited such a light.[7] Those who are intent on discovering man, but do not succeed, should meditate on this truth, because they have been seeking man only in himself.

What is a person? Many may think that the dignity of a person is tied to his independence, to his stability, to the rigidity of his methods, to his power of being a "center" and of setting himself up as a kind of absolute.

Let us look higher. In God there are Persons; and the divine Persons are not like that. *As Persons*, they are not static realities, but are constituted essentially by their relationships.

We may ask ourselves if the most profound interpretation of the created personality may not similarly be a power of relationship with God. In this the person would truly be an image of God, a prolongation of the eternal filiation.[8]

Is not such dependence ennobling? It raises the person far above the philosophical dreams of those who want to make him an immobile center. Our Lord said to his Apostles: "If you loved me, you would have rejoiced because I go to the Father" (Jn 14, 28). If thoughtful men knew how to understand and to desire the true nobility of man, they would not hinder him or detain him, even for the purpose of making him revered. They would sense that his glory consists in movement toward God.

In the same way, the heavenly bodies are not maintained in space except by being attracted to a central sun. Gravitation is a dependence, but makes each planet become a center by its own movement around itself and because other heavenly bodies depend upon it.

The saints achieve this true power of the person. Because they are going toward God, they dominate things that cause others to waver. Sometimes they even rule over irrational creatures. Thus, the reaction of the saints against "self" is a deepening that results in encountering the true source of their person and in freeing it.

At the same time, this enterprise does not cause inhuman tension. It corresponds to the most intimate tendencies of our being and mysteriously satisfies them. It contains a hidden sweetness, and more than a sweetness: it is, at the final stage of the spiritual road, the overflowing cup of which the psalmist sings (see Ps 22, 5); and he who drinks of it no longer has any other thirst.

What are the Seventh Mansions? They are a new and the only real way of loving. We make a mistake when we give the name of love to things that do not deserve to be so named. We form for ourselves a certain idea of the divine lovableness. We think we are responding to it when we transfer part of the best of our feeling toward this transcendence. This is not the way to "love" in the highest sense of the word, that is, to love as Christ loved. To love as Christ loved means to be in a perpetual attitude of giving. What reaches the heart of God is: "The Father loves me, because I lay down my life."[9]

As we have just noted, such an attitude royally fulfills the person, and by that fact puts a created spirit on the level, as it were, of God. Then intimacies become normal, though far removed from sentimental familiarities.

St. John of the Cross says: "Some souls call God their Bridegroom and their Beloved, but he is not really loved by them, because their heart is not whole with him."[10] What does he mean? Is it simply that perfect union may be bought and that we need to pay the price? There is another and more noble meaning: divine friendship requires the soul to present itself before the Lord in the majesty of its person, a majesty that is acquired only by losing oneself.

This is the magnificence of heart that the Scriptures call simplicity: "In the simplicity of my heart I have joyfully offered all these things" (1 Chr 29, 17, Douai). This simplicity, how-

ever, is often misjudged. Job's wife scoffed at him for it. The
world cannot comprehend it, for the world is oriented toward
"self" and does not know the rare and exquisite fruit of the
spirit which is present here.

We ourselves risk making a mistake about the meaning of
simplicity. There is a childish way of understanding the word,
and it is the most ordinary way. We see in "simplicity" a kind
of liberation of nature—of innocent nature, of course. But what
do we mean by innocence? Is it perhaps simply the absence of a
bad disposition, the feeling that "one means well," the poor
innocence of a baby?

We have seen what the saints mean by simplicity. Their interpretation, although quite different, does not locate it in a
far-off paradise. God made us for this simplicity. He made his
blue heavens and his sun to be in conformity with this light. Its
source is found only at the end of a long road. In order to be
acquainted with what we might call the poetry of simplicity,
we must have lived in actuality everything that is signified by
simplicity of heart, and have completely lost ourselves on the
narrow way.

NOTES

1. VII, 3:1.
2. *Ibid.*, 2.
3. *Last Conversations*, May 9, p. 43.
4. *Story of a Soul*, Chap. x, p. 214.
5. See, at the beginning of the works of St. John of the Cross,
   the sketch he designed to represent the ascent of the soul
   toward God.
6. Bernanos used to say: "We live only on the surface of ourselves, and when we go within, it is to die."

7. See *Poems*, VIII, in *Complete Works of St. Teresa of Jesus*, vol III, p. 287, trans. E. Allison Peers. New York: Sheed & Ward 1946.

8. Although the term "Persons" has a special and unique meaning in regard to God, it has been chosen in preference to others. Hence, it is permissible to meditate on the analogical meaning.

9. He immediately adds: ". . . that I may take it up again," for his Resurrection is as essential to his mission as his death; but the following verse shows well that the idea of the *gift* is dominant here: "No one takes it from me . . . I *lay it down* of my own accord" (Jn 10, 17–18).

10. *The Living Flame*, Maxim 82 (Lewis-Zimmerman; Thomas Baker). The Living Flame of Love by St. John of the Cross, translated by David Lewis with an essay by Cardinal Wiseman and additions and an Introduction by Benedict Zimmerman, O.C.D. London: Thomas Baker, 1912.

XXIV
With Christ in God

The substance of the Seventh Mansions from a psychological point of view is this: a way of loving which is love itself, which unites every tendency in simplicity; a clarity of look and heart which is no longer conscious of self.

St. Teresa points out a further aspect, one that we would call more specially "mystical." She says that in these Mansions the souls enjoy the presence of the three divine Persons, in the sense of a full "flowering" which would normally follow the long preparation of the Mansions. No charism may supplant this formation; rather, the charism demands it—even arousing it, intensifying it and accelerating it.

How is life with the "Three" a normal "flowering"? As with all blossoming, it is because there is a promise in the seed. We have been baptized in the name of the Father and of the Son and of the Holy Spirit; we have to fulfill ourselves in this sacramental sign. When will this fulfillment be accomplished? Our Lord tells us very precisely: "If a man loves me . . . my Father will love him; and we will come to him and make our home with him" (Jn 14, 23).

Of course it is not a question of just any kind of love. But, from the instant a soul has received the gift of total love, when Jesus is made Master of all its affections, it follows that his promise must have its full effect. This is the reason the Seventh Mansions normally introduce the soul into the society of the

183

divine Persons. As in all spiritual progress, this is an effect of a gratuitous gift that is simultaneous with interior growth.

Let us look first at the gift. We have just seen that it proceeds from dependence on Christ. In fact, Teresa attests that entrance into the Seventh Mansions has taken place through the intervention of the sacred humanity.[1] In this way she expresses not only the connection between these Mansions and the preceding ones, where, as we have seen, our Lord is equally the principal Agent, but also the constant truth that men have access to the divine mystery only in the Person of the God-Man.

Furthermore, this gift is the communication of the privileges of the divine Person who is the Christ: "Father, I desire that they also whom you gave me, may be with me where I am" (Jn 17, 24). In such a way the instructions and progressions of the Sixth Mansions reach their goal: "Know that I am with you"; "Your mind must be that of Christ." Thus, it is revealed to the Christian under what title and by what way he is to enter into the society of the Three.

"Where I am . . ." that is, in a direct participation in the personal characteristics of the Son. The Christian is already participating in his sonship through grace. Now, by a filial grace that is still more perfect, he is given the gift of being, like the Son, totally inclined "toward the Father." This is the supreme earthly fulfillment of the spiritual life.

Thus the soul first perceives the presence of the divine Persons by becoming conscious of the attitudes communicated to it in Jesus Christ, which are a reflection of their relationships. It is with God because it is present to the Son; toward God, in that it is turned toward the Father by this filial presence; and in God, through the inevitable action of the Holy Spirit in this movement of love.

Is this simple assimilation really what we think of when we read the Gospel and the last chapters of the *Interior Castle*? Perhaps not. To our mind, the presence or the company of someone is a nearness, a proximity that permits us to look at him and converse with him.

This is a material idea. The essence of the divine presence is not in this nearness. Between God and his child proximity in terms of space is not possible. God, "who is working still" (Jn 5, 17), can only become present to a spirit in uniting it to his act.

If the divine Persons let themselves be comprehended, it is by impressing us in their own way. To let themselves be seen means, for them, to grant a fundamental experience in accord with their relationship.

How can there be life and presence in this? A repeated remark of St. Teresa puts us on the right track. Three times she informs us that the Lord introduces the soul into the Seventh Mansion before granting it the grace of the spiritual marriage (a grace which is the same as the Trinitarian grace).[2]

A psychological fact that is attested to with such insistence must be important. Just what does it mean? In a definite way the Seventh Mansions are the "center of the soul" where God makes his abode. A very simple interpretation of this figure would be: through an initial grace that precedes all communication, the soul is permitted to descend into the center of itself, to take complete possession of its powers, and to achieve its unity.

The Sixth Mansions, whose purpose is to form living faith, have prepared this unity, for the powers of the person find their center in faith and their direction through the free choice of their divine "personal" Lord. The unification thus achieved can be called "transformation," for the faculties, acting in concert, reveal their hidden splendor; the intellect is no longer just a simple guide; the will ceases to be uncertain in its fervor. The human act comprises and expresses an authentic "vision." The child of God is now incapable of an act which is not an interior act, and of an act which is not spiritually enlightening.

Sometimes, if it so pleases God, the "sight" of the divine

Persons may go far beyond this vital experience. Teresa says very precisely that the presence of the "Three," in its fullness, has the character of an "intellectual vision." The divine Persons "reveal themselves by some mysterious manifestation of the truth, preceded by an illumination which shines on the spirit like a most dazzling cloud of light.... A sublime knowledge is infused in the soul, imbuing it with the certainty of the truth that the Three are of one substance, power, and knowledge, and are one God. Thus, that which we hold as a doctrine of faith, the soul now, so to speak, understands *by sight.*"[3]

There is a fundamental grace, a kind of grace of state which is also Trinitarian; and when God so wills, St. Teresa says, there springs from this grace of an excess of enlightenment. The first grace is more substantial; the second more theological. We might tend to misunderstand the first of these two graces, because our idea of these Mansions may be a little theatrical, when in reality they are but the completely fulfilled Christian life, and the soul "is hid with Christ in God" (Col 3, 3), according to the program of St. Paul. If union with the holy Trinity is "transforming," certainly this is true through that which is most substantial in it.

"Hid in God": In these three words both the humility of this state and its nobility are expressed. The soul's interior acts are immense, because it cut through appearances and all superficiality on the day when Christ Jesus, and then the holy Trinity, revealed themselves to its "interior" through a hitherto unknown deepening. Henceforth every step will be taken in the orbit of the Three, which will make the soul run with ease "from end to end mightily" (Wis 8:1 Douai).

"Hid in God," but "with Christ": we must not lose sight of this condition. We are not raised to this great divine mystery by leaving Christ behind, but are introduced to it by a profound life with Christ, for he is the "Way" (Jn 14, 6).

This sanctuary of the glorious Trinity to which we are all

invited is the sheepfold of which he is the Door. Let his own "go in" or "go out"; they shall "find pasture" (Jn 10, 9). For, according to St. Teresa, the soul here "goes in and goes out" freely, passing from action to contemplation. She is not in a state of rapture which would absorb her. On the contrary, "she is more ardent than ever in all that concerns God's service."[4]

Is this not a proof that the gift of living with the Three, which is directly related to our vocation as baptized Christians, is normal in the Christian life? Nothing is more simple or more humble, as we shall see, than its perfect flowering.

NOTES

1. On this point the sober lines of the *Interior Castle* are completed by spiritual testimonies 25. Collected Works of St. Teresa, Vol. I.
2. "Our Lord . . . introduces (this soul) into his own Mansion, which is the Seventh" (VII, 1:3). There is the same affirmation in almost identical terms in VII, 1:7, and 2:12.
3. VII, 1:9.
4. VII, 1:11.

XXV
He Goes Before You to Galilee

The mystery that Christ accomplishes in his elect in the Seventh Mansions is silent and hidden, like all his mysteries. There is nothing pretentious, nothing to dazzle the imagination, no more than there was in the Incarnation, accomplished in the unknown village of Nazareth, or in the Resurrection, which awakened no one in Jerusalem.

St. Teresa uses rather sober words when she speaks of the presence of the divine Persons, noting that this elevated grace does not disturb everyday life. A vision would excite the soul, a rapture would certainly be noticed. The indescribable nearness of the Three Persons transcends the domain of emotion. Is the sublimity of their presence beyond expression? Not at all; it is manifested, but in a restrained manner.

Did not Jesus exceed every splendor in his earthly life because of his true greatness? In his risen life he retains his taste for hiddenness: His encounters with others are sedate and he manifests a humble attitude; even his program is announced in few words: He "is going before you to Galilee" (Mt 28, 7). Galilee is the place of his childhood, of his silence and obscurity. Those who have been "raised up ... with Christ," who "seek," who set their hearts on things that are above (Col 3, 1–2), live their new life in secret, as it were, "hid now with Christ."

The four chapters of the Seventh Mansions, especially the

last, portray this trait with a delightful precision. Their author hides neither the fullness, nor the depth, nor the supreme height of such a life. Yet, the final word is one of Christian humility, not indeed like a musical flat that softens a tone, but as the perfect expression of these very lofty realities.

We look in her teaching for traces, reflections, and signs in daily life of the Trinitarian grace that characterizes the Seventh Mansions, so that we may understand what makes up the transformation effected by this grace. These effects are delicately shaded with restraint, even those that are going to "awaken" feeling.

Life in the interior of the soul—in its "center"—tends to manifest itself in feeling, for God has willed it to do so. How? By "certain secret intuitions," by an "impulse" which is "usual" and "frequent" and delightful, sweetly, by a "penetrating touch," and in a "profound silence."[1]

It is sufficient to explain these things in a brief way, for they are meant to be experienced—and few experience them. It will be more useful for us to meditate on the second great sign: "transformation." This is the life of virtue which is presented as the final word of the doctrine of the *Castle*. What is the significance of St. Teresa's concluding doctrine? First of all it teaches us that there are virtues and virtues. As always, the soul has to exercise itself in virtue, and it does not reach this final stage without having acquired solid ones.

But, beyond virtues that are practiced through tension (and sometimes even through pretention), beyond even the raptures of self-sacrifice and abnegation which go hand in hand with spiritual progress, there is a way of virtue which is proper to "the soul God chooses for his special dwelling place." "How forgetful of her ease, and how far from seeking man's esteem should she be! . . . *all* her thoughts are bent on how to please him better, and when, and how she can show the love she bears him."[2] Here are found the foundations of a humility and a sacrifice that are fixed in the center of the soul at a depth hitherto unknown; and, from this source, all the Christian virtues spring with an incomparable vigor.

Nevertheless, work is not precluded, and, in this regard, the attainment of these virtues proceeds along the same lines as all the others. This may seem surprising, but it is a point on which the Saint insists—almost impatiently so. Her last pages clamor for "works," which are simply acts of humble virtue: master your will; strive to be "the least of all and the slave of others, watching how you can please and help them"; work to "acquire the virtues and practice them."[3]

Is she directing her words to some rash soul who would lay claim to the graces of the Seventh Mansions without having deserved to enter them? Not at all. She immediately makes it clear that she is not speaking to beginners, but to those who receive the "aspirations and communications" proper to these Mansions.[4] In fact, she has noted that these aspirations are "love letters" that demand an answer, and that by them the soul is disposed to answer with a generous will.[5]

Appeals, dispositions—an act must still be accomplished. One may be tempted to prefer tranquility; this seems to be the tendency of "all who are held in the body." These "aspirations" also wage war on the powers and senses—a "fierce war." Thus, St. Teresa explains the necessity of moral effort even in this area of fulfillment.

To think the contrary would be to forget that earth is not heaven, and that in one way or another the members of the Church on earth belong to the Church militant. Teresa herself, at the summit of holiness, close to her death, had to triumph over a strong, interior resistance in order to submit to the order of a superior.

Hence, she urges her children on, even when they may believe themselves to be secure and sheltered within, because for her the Seventh Mansions are not an absolute of perfection.

Some negligence is still possible; as always, progress is still necessary. The thought that we have reached the goal may cause us to lose everything. Shortly before her death, St. Therese of Lisieux confided that if she were to believe herself capable of practicing a virtue, she felt she would be lost.[6]

These are the humble aspects of genuine greatness. Now, let us consider what is truly great in these virtues and how they correspond to the state of spiritual fulfillment. They correspond to it in that they are the expression of the soul's interior orientation, as well as its guarantee and support. It is still a question of going to the Father, but like Christ and in the Spirit of Christ. For Jesus says: "For this reason the Father loves me, because I lay down my life" (Jn 10, 17).

The humble virtues accomplish this: They make the perfect Christian "the slave of God" and "the slave of others,"[7] something sold for the salvation of the world as Christ "was himself sold."[8] And they do this without romanticism, without even directly aiming beyond their immediate surroundings. "Do you think," says St. Teresa, "it is a trifling matter that your humility and mortification, your readiness to serve your sisters, your fervent charity toward them, and your love of God, should be as a fire to enkindle their zeal, and that you should incite them to imitate you in your constant practice of the other virtues?"[9]

Here is a peak of contemplation, the summit on which the Incarnate Word lived his life of obedience and sacrifice. In reality, it is the interior act asserting itself, reaching out and becoming incarnate. It comes from the spirit and from the substance of love.

God has willed to make his eternal act overflow on his creatures. The soul that is totally united to him cannot do otherwise than associate itself with this action. It is God's servant, ready for all his works.

It is this fact that gives so profound a tone to the *fiat* of the Blessed Virgin and to many of the words of the saints; for

example, those of St. Therese of the Child Jesus: "I wish to
spend my heaven in doing good upon earth!"[10] How nice that
is, we think. But it is something far grander: it is the contemplative way attaining its goal. By this the soul is established in
common life in a new way. Perfect contemplation is not a gaze
that separates one from ordinary life; rather, it is one that con-
tinually follows its Lord by means of the common things of life.

Consequently, there is nothing surprising if everything is
very unassuming in appearance. Teresa is most profound when
she brings the spiritual ascent she has been describing to this
conclusion. Indeed, she is evangelical, for according to the
Gospel, the Christian virtues are the proper language of love:
"If you love me, you will keep my commandments" (Jn 14, 15).

Now we begin to see the spiritual substance contained in true
forgetfulness of self, and in the gift of one's heart to the
neighbor. We begin to understand that the sensible effects of
the Sixth Mansions were only preparations. These quiet initiatives succeed the strong vibrations of emotion like rain following the wind and the storm. Great stirrings of the atmosphere
are not the fruitful ones; their use is to bring the gentle rain,
silent and penetrating.

In the same way, there must be a kind of condensation in the
soul: the vapors must settle and the whirlwinds be concen-
trated, so that following the example of the divine life, its life
may be all fruitfulness: I am working (Jn 5, 17), says the Lord.

There are virtues and virtues. We can guess the quality of the
virtue we are speaking of here. It differs greatly from those we
try to practice in the purity and integrity of its interior movement. Take, for example, zeal. There are so many ways of exercising this virtue. We need a perfect love of God to practice it in
the maternal and virginal way proposed by our Saint: to sacrifice ourselves without words and without showing it, for the
good of God in souls—for souls who may be close to us, whose
progress may be imperceptible, who, at any rate, will not

understand this fraternal self-sacrifice. In zeal of this kind, everything comes from God and goes only to God.

This humble self-sacrifice is the final scene given to us by St. Teresa at the very end of the most sublime of her writings. Souls who are truly great make no noise. St. Paul knew that his Christians were an elite, even a spectacle to all. By what sign were they to be known? It was to be by a disposition that the Vulgate characterizes by "modestia," a rather untranslatable word that is variously rendered.[11] It evokes the idea of a beautiful moral harmony: of moderation, good balance, justice, kind and affable restraint—as much a quality of charm as of gravity. At the same time it also signifies self-effacement and silence.

Why this attitude? "The Lord is at hand" (Phil 4, 5) explains the Apostle. For Paul as for Teresa, the divine nearness imposes an eminent degree of humble restraint. Moreover, Teresa is logical in representing the Christian virtues as the fruit of the highest graces. All preceding graces—even extraordinary ones—are less extraordinary than a perfect virtue accomplished by human determination.

She knows, and intimates to us, that the end product of our progress here is precisely a psychological structure from which true virtue may proceed. This is the Kingdom of God *within*. An effect of this structure that merits special notice is the attitude toward suffering. At the summit of which we are speaking, there are "struggles, suffering, and fatigue," but they do not take away peace.[12] There is even "a strong desire for suffering,"[13] but "this does not disturb her peace," for the soul is now wholly given over to the divine good pleasure.

This is a characteristic of St. Teresa's teaching: Suffering in this life has the value of an end in reference to the highest graces. "To be truly spiritual," she says, "is to be branded with his mark, which is the cross."[14] Her last admonition sounds the same note: "During the brief time this life lasts . . . let us give our Lord every sacrifice we can, both interior and exterior, and he will deign to unite it to his own."[15]

When his disciples asked for glory, Christ answered: "are you able to drink the cup that I am to drink?" (Mt 20, 22). The important thing is to acquire the power to do this—that is to attain to the particular degree of charity that puts a soul on the level of the Savior's sacrifice. Otherwise, it cannot be on the level of the Gospel. This is the reason why the Seventh Mansions are not just something added, a luxury. They are necessary for the integrity of the Christian life.

NOTES

1. VII, 2:7; 3:7; 3:9.
2. VII, 4:9.
3. VII, 4:11, 13.
4. VII, 3:8.
5. We catch the realism of St. Teresa in this passage; even in the state of "consummate" union with God, the response of the will is demanded by ever-renewed appeals which require courage (see VII, 4:15).
6. See *Last Conversations*, August, p. 140.
7. VII, 4:12, 13.
8. VII, 4:13.
9. VII, 4:22.
10. *Last Conversations*, July 17, p. 102.
11. The New American has "unselfishness"; Jerusalem Bible names it "tolerance"; the Revised American edition gives "moderation"; Spenser translates it "forbearance"; Ronald Knox uses "courtesy."
12. VII, 2:24.
13. VII, 3:4.
14. VII, 4:12.
15. VII, 4:23.

XXVI
That Your Joy May Be Full

If charity reaches its full beauty in the Seventh Mansions (as far as is possible in this world), then joy must do the same. Hence, it may be helpful to think a little about Christian joy.

Joy—no quality is more commonly dissembled. It is something everybody desires, but does anyone know exactly what it is? Does any blessing need more analysis in order to distinguish it from those that resemble it? Is there any whose deepest reality is more hidden?

We make much today of the joyous exuberance of youth. We rightly see it as a sign and factor of health, even of moral health. Yet, there is a great distance between their vivacity and true joy. The superficialities that can be hidden in enthusiasms may even deceive us for a long time. The joy of nature and of learning, when carried over into religious life, may not ring entirely true, even though it is healthy in itself, even though we make an effort to transpose it to a supernatural plane.

In trying to understand joy, it may be of help to think of it in its highest degree—the joy of heaven. For many of us, heaven is the possession of what we have desired, the recovery of what we have lost, the reward for what we have sacrificed—satisfactions without risk. On a higher level, heaven is the greatness and perfection of our being confirmed forever, a circle of glory and moral beauty forming itself around "self."

But, we know that beyond these blessings there is something

still greater: the possession of God. Yet, even this high ideal fails to express the essential form of our joy, for the creature is still too much the center. The Gospel does not show us heaven under this form. It contains no notion of our taking possession of the Lord; instead, it speaks of our sharing in his joy (see Mt 25, 21–23).

God's joy is his very life, his eternal gift. To share in his joy is to share in this eternal act. We are dynamic beings, made as we are in the image of God. We become such more truly through Christ who makes of us, with himself, an impulse toward the Father. In this impulse, we enter into the divine activity and into the true joy of our Christian vocation.

The joy of heaven is not repose (in the sense in which repose is conceived as cessation from work). Yet, it is repose in the sense in which God himself rests: in the perfection of his activity. The same is true of the elect: Their repose and their joy, their "eternal rest," is the perfection of their movement toward God, which is participation in the divine life. Only in heaven can this repose be given, for only in heaven will our power of acting be total, capable of becoming completely open and fully efficacious.

The perfect spiritual *act* is our end—joy, even the holy joy of heaven which accompanies it, is not an end. This idea may be a little rarefied for our imaginations. But try to understand: Joy cannot be an end; of its very essence it is not meant to be an end. The moment the movement toward God would stop to rest in itself, in that self-same moment joy would disappear.

God did not create us to live in a prison, even a prison of happiness; and our joy, like our center, is always outside ourselves. Here again we turn to St. Teresa's words: "All my life I live in Thee."[1] We find in her a doctrine of joy that tends toward forgetfulness of self. For the great St. Teresa as well as for the little Therese, all that counts is love. But she is also human. She is not a teacher of "pure love." For her, the pri-

macy of love is a need of the heart, not the requirement of a
system. Inundated as she was with ineffable joys, she makes
much of this gift of joy. She welcomes it to the full, and promises it with assurance.

Exactly what does she promise? Not the delights of heaven,
although she seems to have tasted something of them. She even
assures us that, in the Seventh Mansions, "the glory enjoyed by
the saints is no longer the object of the soul's desire."² She
promises those things that will lead us toward heavenly bliss.
The proposal is made to all Christians. The ordinary joys of this
world are normal and desirable; however, none of them are
authentic if they do not tend toward "perfect joy." In the perfect joy announced by the Lord, we may distinguish three elements: expectation, flight, sacrifice.

"Blessed are they who *hunger* and *thirst* for righteousness"
(Mt 5, 6), says the Lord. He does not say: "Blessed are they who
are righteous" for then who would dare lay claim to joy? But
joy is certain when the heart has become entirely a hunger for
righteousness—for holiness.

It does not imply something completed, but something
opened: "with open mouth I pant, because I long for your
commandments." (Ps 119, 131). The heart breathes joyously
through opening itself completely. This joy is a *quest*: "Seek
the things that are above" (Col 3, 1); "like newborn babes, long
for the pure spiritual milk" (1 Pt 2, 2).

These texts radiate paschal joy. Are not the Resurrection and
the new birth the condition of becoming open? We notice that,
while the Church says to us during Advent, "Rejoice,"³ at Easter she says, "Seek."⁴ How true it is that on earth joy is expectation and expectation joy.

Then St. Peter says: What saves you now is an "appeal to God
for a clear conscience, through the resurrection of Jesus Christ"
(1 Pt 3, 21). We always discover the Resurrection to be a foundation, always an attitude of seeking. *Salvation*, the happiness

of the spirit, is first of all a conscious and confident poverty. We
are conscious of being at the bottom, otherwise we would not
seek the milk that makes us grow. Right desire is conscious that
it is not yet moral beauty, so it too "petitions God."

From this poverty, not simply endured but accepted, arises
the confident appeal of redeemed humanity. It is an appeal, not
an assurance. For this reason, the spiritual certitudes of this
world are not without shadows. Faith has its own obscurities.
"Good intention" and "good will" are not completely sure ref-
uges. The equilibrium of great souls leaves room for combats,
and even peace admits of anxieties.

In the midst of these shadows is joy, for nothing is closed off,
and that is the essential thing. For one who seeks justice, it is
enough that the "gates of righteousness" (Ps 118, 19) be open,
and that flight be possible. For joy in this life is still the jubilation of going out from self, the radiant smile of the "spirit"
which makes it escape, as St. John of the Cross notes so well:
"Forth unobserved I went, Oh! happy lot!"⁵

In truth, the spirit is here in its essential joy: movement toward God. This is the joy the Psalmist dreams of when he
envies the dove: "O that I had wings like a dove! I would fly
away and be at rest" (Ps 55, 6). Flight and rest—for him they are
all one. This is why hunger, flight, seeking, expectation and the
ardent desire, although they seem like distress, become happiness when it is the "spirit" which assumes them. For then they
are spiritual activity, which, according to the divine will, must
fill, make valid and beautify our lives. The spirit of the soul
becomes one same thing with God.⁶

When the "spirit" seeks, it is never frustrated. For it, to seek
is to find—to find, not in hope, but immediately, really. Thus,
even in this life, it finds exactly what it desires, although not in
the same way as in heaven: It finds the perfect gift, the clear
choice—and for it this is already beatitude.⁷ "I really don't see
what I'll have after death that I don't already possess in this

life," said St. Therese of the Child Jesus in the most sorrowful period of her life. "I shall see God, true; but as far as being in his presence, I am totally there here on earth."[8] Her soul was suffering; her spirit, like the dove, was flying away and was at rest.

There is another way of entering into the mystery of joy, no less mysterious, and one that the saints have all known and practiced: the way of suffering. We have already remarked that to open oneself is the source of life and of joy. What shall we say when the heart, in breaking itself, in losing itself, opens itself completely? Jesus himself experienced this sorrow: "For the joy that was set before him [he] endured the cross" (Heb 12, 2).

Joy was proposed to Christ in the sense that it was offered by right to the all-holy will of the "immortal King of ages." He submits to the cross, not to refuse joy but in order to encounter it. We see the Father presenting to the new Adam, as he had to the first, the perspective of an expanding joy, and the Son turning himself to the cross in a docile spirit in view of the joy which he desires with all his heart. More clear-sighted than the first man, the Redeemer knew that a creature achieves his beatitude only through renouncing it. He himself will say: "Was it not necessary that the Christ should suffer these things and enter into his glory?" (Lk 24, 26).

If we stop to think about it, we can comprehend his choice. Is it not the essential joy of the sacred humanity to spend itself to the utmost in order to be as true an instrument and as exact an expression of the divinity as possible? And was there not something overwhelming in being used for a purpose so replete with holiness and generosity, in being used to express infinite love? Yet, if he wished to have a joy worthy of him, it was necessary that he should aspire to this near annihilation. In point of fact, he cried out in eager longing for his sacrifice: "I have a baptism to be baptized with, and now I am constrained until it is accomplished" (Lk 12, 50); "I have earnestly desired to eat the

Passover" (Lk 22, 15). The evangelists have indeed done well
to set down these words which reveal (although in necessarily
common terms) what might be called the friction of the two
natures, and how the human nature, in order to find its joy,
had to claim the cross.

It will always be thus for Christians, according to the measure of their nearness to their Master and of their desire to be
yet nearer. For all of us, our possession of Christian joy depends
on whether we are or are not at the level of life and love where
he awaits us. Because we are on a level of joy, we need to
enlarge the conclusion we made at the end of the preceding
meditation. Holy suffering in this world is closely bound to the
depths of joy, because it breaks down the barriers of self.

"Are you able to drink the cup that I am to drink?" (Mt 20,
22). His is a bitter chalice that overflows and becomes sweet.[9]
To be able to suffer means to be able to rejoice also, but with a
joy that is no longer on the plane of earthly joys. The difference
between ordinary joys and this joy is not simply a quantative
one. This perfect joy is quite another thing, something the
"world" cannot understand: a liberation from desire. The
world pictures heaven as a reward with interest compounded:
Abraham, in regaining his son Isaac, has the good things he has
sacrificed restored—in a word, the sacrifice itself annulled.

But we ought to remember that we are no longer using the
outlook of the Old Testament. When God asks for an "Isaac"
now, it is not with a view of returning it. Or, if it is restored, it is
not in order to revive the lost joy, but in order to bring about a
higher joy, the fruit of a sacrifice that has been accepted without hope of return.

Consider what happened, at a depth we cannot fathom, after
Our Lady and St. Joseph found Jesus in the Temple. They did
not go back to Nazareth just as they had left it, with the added
solace of a trial that had ended well. To be sure, Jesus was with
them, but henceforth his destiny as victim was definite. The joy

of his presence would never again be what it had been up until
then. In this itself we see progress; Jesus revealed to them a new
depth in his total dedication to the Father so that they could
unite their own will to his. This new depth would be the source
of yet greater joys which, from that time on, would sustain the
holy Virgin.

Such, it seems, is perfect joy here below: not something permanent, but an impulse; differing from eternal joy by its in-
completeness, yet like it through its objective activity. To just
such a joy the Gospel invites us: "Ask and you will receive, that
your joy may be full" (Jn 16, 24). For what should we ask? Our
Lord does not tell us here exactly what to ask for; but knowing
our Father, we also know that everything is contained in asking
for the Kingdom of God.[10]

The Gospel tells us further that this Kingdom is received
within us. This means that divine sovereignty is established in
the very center of the soul and serves as a base for a whole
psychological category that the Gospel sums up as his justice.
We shall ask for the Kingdom of God; we shall receive the grace
of wholly directing ourselves to the Lord in every part of our
being. Then our joy will be full. St. Matthew even promises an
excess.

The saints were acquainted with the full measure of this true
joy as well as with all its extra benefits. It is offered to everyone:
"Ask and you shall receive!" This is both a commandment and
a firm assurance. It suffices for us to accomplish the condition,
which is charity.

It is the joy of the Apostles: It was first promised and given to
them. They were not without sorrows or perplexities or errors,
but they "left . . . rejoicing" (Acts 5, 41).

It is the joy of the Church on earth. And the perfume of this
joy is the praise which she expresses in the liturgy. Praise is the
fullness of joy exhaled by charity, the musical form of movement toward God. The Church sings because she is completely

carried away in this movement. Indeed, if the measure of each
Christian's happiness is not full, because he has not enough
love, the Church has this mighty joy in which she wants each of
her children to share. While each is waiting to attain his own
joy, and in order to help himself in the task, each can and ought
to participate in the common treasure.

The better the Christian understands the profound meaning
of liturgical joy, the more he will enter into it—into the expectation that it offers, the flight it inspires, the sacrifice that is its
home. For at the center of our liturgy is the "Holy Sacrifice." It
is joy because it is the effusion of charity, drawing from charity
its definitive meaning, that of the Meal where the children of
God nourish their life in joyful security. The more the heart of
the Christian has penetrated the reality of the sacrifice, the
more he will share in the happiness of this table, for he will
taste the divine charity which is its delight. If the liturgical
celebrations were supposed to nourish Christians only through
a kind of musical exaltation, however well based on Scripture,
many, indeed some of the best, would find it insufficient. Once
past the age of childhood, there are so many sorrowful notes in
a Christian life! By making the Memorial of his Passion a banquet, Jesus teaches his own how to make their praise spring
from sacrifice, how to encounter in sacrifice his own divine
fullness, how to incarnate the joy of heaven in our earthly
condition—in other words, how to make the sacramental encounter human and authentic.

The liturgy completes the mystery of the true friends of our
Lord. When we reach this level we grasp and magnify the joy
of the Church; we accomplish the conciliar decrees to the
full. Built on this foundation each one's joy is completely
secure. Is it not to those who have walked the way of his passion that Jesus says: Your "joy, no one will take from you"
(Jn 16, 22)?

NOTES

1. *Poems*, ii, p. 281, vol. III, Peers ed.
2. vii, 3:5.
3. Entrance Hymn, iii Sunday of Advent.
4. "Seek the things that are above" (Easter Vigil Mass).
5. *Dark Night*, Stanza 1.
6. vii, 2:6. The distinction which St. Teresa makes between the soul and the spirit of the soul should not be likened to the opposition that exists in the Fifth Mansions between the lower faculties and the will. Here, there is no opposition, only a shade of meaning: that of a specialized function in the being which chooses and lives in it.
7. A philosopher would say: a spirit is a form and is nourished by formal acts.
8. *Last Conversations*, May 15, p. 45.
9. "My cup overflows" (Ps 23, 5); the context sufficiently shows that a cup of *joy* is meant.
10. "Seek first his kingdom" (Mt 6, 33).

XXVII

At the Sources of the Spiritual
Marriage

Perfect union of the soul with God is often represented under the symbol of marriage. We may sometimes grow a little weary of this image, which even St. Teresa employs. It has been used in religious imagery and in "pious" literature to the point of insipidity.

Nevertheless, it rests on Scripture and on the Liturgy. Indeed, the Church makes such official use of it that we may well ask if it is not something more than a symbol, if it may not even express a mysterious reality. But what reality? First of all, in this union where the soul is bride, who is the bridegroom? Is it the divinity itself, as the language of the mystics gives us to understand? Is it the Person of our Lord, as the Church expresses it in the words, *Spouse of Christ?*

St. Teresa adopts both interpretations, which cannot be by chance. What then is the exact relation between them? We can scarcely get a complete idea of the Seventh Mansions unless we try to answer these questions.

Perhaps the simplest way to answer them will be to reflect upon the spiritual meaning of marriage in its institution. From that we shall be able to grasp God's idea, which will furnish us with a true insight, for, as the psalm tells us: "The counsel of the Lord stands forever" (Ps 33, 11).

Even before God took Eve from Adam's side, he was careful

to manifest his precise reason for doing so, by defining the wife through her relation to her husband (and vice versa, of course) as "... a helpmate" (Gn 2, 18, Jerusalem). A helpmate—the word must be given a very broad meaning. It is not simply a question of the assistance that can be rendered a man through collaboration in his material duties. Nor can it be limited to that most essential cooperation which consists in being mother to his descendants; more fundamental still than transmitting his life is living his life, for one can only give what one has. Therefore, for husband and wife, helping each other will be a way of self-fulfillment for each.

The first emphasis, then, is on a spiritual cooperation, for the principal reality willed by God in his new creature is the spirit. In fact, to possess any good whatsoever without tending through that good toward the sovereign good is an animal act. The ray of sunshine makes an animal glad by the simple contact of warmth. Besides making a man glad for the same reason, it arouses in him the notion and delight of light, which is something more. But if this good he possesses is a being like himself, in all the fullness of spiritual beauty, what will this normally arouse in his soul but the sense of the infinite and of the need of God? And if it were given to him as his own, what will he find in possessing it according to the spirit except God himself? Thus, to receive and give back the gift of a soul, is, so to speak, to drink at a fount filled with God. Here we see the human milieu becoming a celestial road—we see the "spiritual" marriage.

By reflecting on this primary aspect of spiritual marriage, we get an idea of how, according to the creative idea, human affections are a pure and holy canal, made to empty themselves into God. The love God was meant to circulate organically in the family of Adam, achieving a living unity without any violence. Without any violence because without any rivalry, for the Lord, being the supreme end would enter into all legitimate ends. Could created love fear to go astray in establishing itself where

Love the Creator had first made a home? Perfectly ordered and always in agreement with its essential inclination, created love could only grow in vigor and in precision through encountering God in the special objects chosen by God.

Such was God's plan: to inject his own love into human love in order that there might be more love in the world and, in all love, more beauty. In this plan the heart of man is swallowed up in God's love. However, our first parents did not know the "spiritual marriage" because they did not fulfill its conditions, so we have still to ask how God wants it to be lived now. He has given us his Son, the new Adam, so that through him we might be offered this union according to the spirit. Admirable as was the first divine idea, even more admirable is its renewal.

But why was such a substitution necessary? Could not God reestablish order without making his Son intervene? The theologians say that, from a moral point of view, the answer is "yes"; if there is question only of the fault, he is master of his pardon.

From the psychological view, however, the problem is not so simple, even for the Almighty. To justify means to create charity. It is easy for God to create. But if the one he wishes to establish in his love says "no," who will take away this "no"? God cannot do it without the creature's consent, for charity is either a free act or it is not charity; the creature himself cannot do it, for his refusal keeps him imprisoned. He allowed the power of his will to be lost, through being unfaithful to his duty; and what was worse, he perverted and wasted the power for love that his free will is. Could he receive a new effusion of grace when in this state?

Christ seems to indicate that he could not. When speaking of the New Law succeeding the Old, he uses a comparison familiar to his audience: "No one puts new wine into old wineskins" (Mt 9, 17; Lk 5, 37), a truth which can be equally applied to infusing grace into fallen man.

When St. Paul speaks of the "old man," he is alluding, like

the Lord, to congenital decay, the fruit of sin: a psyche without wings; the fear of leaving self or of going beyond self; the refusal to scale difficulties—in short the mentality of an old man, holding back before the challenge of charity (see Rom 6, 6; Eph 4, 22; Col 3, 10).

We have all received this debilitated nature from our parents. It is not capable by itself of carrying the weight of supernatural life, for grace is not a reality independent of nature. It is grafted upon nature; it assumes nature's resources. Being divine life, the least it can exact of the nature to which it must be united is integrity. How could it give itself to a degraded nature?

Through his holy humanity, the Savior is substituted for sinful humanity; through the power of his divinity, he is incorporated into it. The evident conclusion of this is that our first relationship with our Lord is a filial one. He is the unique source of our life of grace. We could say that he is the Father and Mother of all Christians.

Notice that Christ himself lays claim to this paternal aspect of his mission. He even seems anxious to establish the fact. Several times in the Gospel he emphasizes that his own relationship with his Father is the pattern of our relationship with him.[1] "As . . . I live because of the Father, so he who eats me, will live because of me" (Jn 6, 57); may they "become perfectly one so that the world may know . . . that you have loved them *even as* you have loved me" (Jn 17, 23); I know my [sheep] and my own know me *as* the Father knows me and I know the Father" (Jn 10, 14–15).

Nowhere does the paternity of Christ appear more clearly than in his sacrifice. There his love for us is carried to its utmost limits, reproducing in an ineffable manner the love of the Father for his only Son. When the world sees its Savior suffering, it realizes that he has "loved his own as much as the Father has loved him." It is a real paternity: Catholic tradition from the time of Origen assures us that the Church was born from the side of the Savior when it was opened by a lance.

Just as the Son comes forth from the Father, so also the
Church comes forth from Christ. It follows that, just as the Son
returns to the Father in the Holy Spirit, so also, in the same
Holy Spirit, Christians are to give themselves to Christ. When
the return of redeemed souls to the Savior reaches its peak of
perfection, is this not simply the "spiritual marriage"? Here
again the Fathers, following St. John, portray the Church not
only as "daughter" of Christ, but also as "spouse."

The relation of Father to child, of spouse to his bride, the one
flowing from the other: this is the total concept of the relationship between Christ and his own.

Christ presents himself to Christians as Spouse, not simply
because it is the human symbol that can best depict his perfect
love for us, but rather in order that this relationship may not
remain unfulfilled. St. Teresa recognizes this symbol to be a
very imperfect one, for, she points out: "I make this comparison
because there is no more suitable one."[3]

The idea of "spiritual marriage" takes on immense dimensions when we view it from this height. We are apt to think of it
today as a state reserved to consecrated virgins. Certainly they
are "spouses of Christ" by a special title. But when St. Paul
wrote to the Corinthians, he addressed himself to *all the faithful* of the city: "Many of you are weak and ill, and some have
died (1 Cor 11, 30). His words: "I have espoused you to one
Husband" (2 Cor 11, 2 Douai), were spoken to all.

"Believing in Christ" ought to mean to everyone "going all
the way to the end of the road." We know well that the world's
sin lies not in offering him this magnanimous faith (see Jn 16,
8–9). We run the risk of sharing in this sin by being content
with a spiritual horizon that is too limited, by a truncated
understanding of our Christian vocation, by a badly conceived
sense of reverence, and by a kind of slothful reserve. All these
are reasons why too many of the faithful do not make the
kind of complete response to the new Adam that he asks of
them.

NOTES

1. The comparison our Savior proposes needs to be developed with some discernment: We must refrain from putting the relationship of the Son of God with his Father on the same level (which in theological language is "notional"), as that of the Incarnate Word with men. The distance between them is infinite. The comparison, however, is made by Jesus himself with clarity and insistence. We need neither avoid it nor minimize it.

2. In this context especially, the phrases "as" and "even as" are, in the mouth of Christ, the supreme word of revelation. We should note that, whether it concerns his relationship with his own or of Christians with each other, he does not say only "as Us", but "in Us," which is something still greater.

3. She uses it especially to represent the indissolubility that characterizes the union of the Seventh Mansions. This privilege may seem to make the "spiritual marriage" a closed state, but above and beyond it there opens out to the Christian an immense pattern of progress according to the similitude proposed by Jesus. In light of this, we lay aside our naive view of the Seventh Mansions as an accomplished state of perfection. We see in them simply the condition of the new life which should always be growing while we are in earth until it reaches its final fulfillment in heaven.

XXVIII
Spouse of Christ

What is the "spiritual marriage" in practice, when our Lord Jesus Christ is the Bridegroom? Many sentimental answers can be given, but the essential one will spring from what has been noted in the preceding chapter. We must look very high if we want to learn what it really means to be the spouse of Christ. Very high—for we have to picture the divine relationship of the Father and the Son.

The Son of God receives himself from the Father (a relationship which, in the present context, can be called "filial"), and directs himself totally toward the Father in the Holy Spirit, through a movement which is identical with that of the Father toward him. Because this is the model of all spiritual union, we venture to call it, in a typical sense, "spousal."

"As the Father has loved me," said the Incarnate Word, "so I have loved you." The immediate meaning of this is confirmed by everything that our Savior gave us in his earthly existence and in his sacrifice: "Greater love has no man than this, that a man lay down his life for his friends" (Jn 15, 13). Just as the Father gives himself wholly to his Son, so also the Son of God made Man gives himself wholly to men.

It follows that we must love him in return as he loves his Father. This is the lofty and essential form of the love which makes a redeemed creature the spouse of Christ.

As he loves his father means: completely. And this completeness in some ways contains his whole being. If it did not, it would not be the Holy Spirit; for if the love of the Father and the Son were less than their being, their love would not be God. Therefore, the great virtue of the spouse is the integrity of love. Integrity and virginity are one and the same. St. Paul is characterizing the virgin when he says she is *not divided* (see 1 Cor 7, 32–33). If the Son loves his Father with a virginal love, he, the God-Man, likewise wishes to be loved with complete integrity. The Gospel loudly proclaims his demand and his right to be preferred to everything, to be chosen out of everything, to be followed to the limits of total sacrifice. This is the right of the Bridegroom (see Mt 10, 37).

Consequently, the Christian program exacts spiritual virginity from everyone. St. Paul testifies to this, as we have seen, when he writes to the Christians of Corinth: "I have espoused you to one husband, that I may present you as a chaste virgin to Christ" (2 Cor 11, 2 Douai).

Heaven is the full flowering of this essential and total relationship of souls to Christ: in our present life, spiritual virginity means living wholly committed to God, and really flourishes only in the Seventh Mansions. In heaven, each of the elect will be a chosen one, an only one, without rival—the very word "elect" means this. Can this glorious singularity exist in this world? Of course; based, however, not on childish pretensions of sentiment, but on that quality of dedication to God that is the whole of true life. The completely supernatural decision is an act which is so singularly singular! It constitutes the "person" in his highest dignity: the spirit centered on God thereby becomes a center and in some way stands erect on the level of its Lord, high above that of "self."

If the quality of spouse is so special, why does the Church seem so prodigal with this title, giving it without distinction to the virgins she consecrates? How can St. Paul say to the whole assembly of his faithful: "I have espoused you to one husband?"

Perhaps a little clarification is needed. Neither in St. Paul's words nor in the "Come, Spouse of Christ" of the Bishop when giving the veil to nuns, is there any question of espousals in the real sense. "Spouse" here does not mean the espoused one, but the promise of becoming one. If we do not take the Apostle and the Church as saying what they are not saying, the meaning is clear. There are not two ways of attaining to perfect union with Christ. The words of St. Teresa remain the great principle without in any way contradicting the declarations of the liturgy: "Before consummating the celestial marriage, (he) brings (the soul) into the Seventh Mansions."[1] We need only distinguish between the promise of marriage and the marriage itself in order to see the harmony.

The promise, or the official presentation of the betrothed, is an act of the Church; perfect union is a gift of God, which presupposes the accomplishment of a moral and psychological preparation. No exterior act, not even if it consecrates a fervent intention, can replace the interior fulfillment.

To stress this exact meaning of "Come, Spouse of Christ," does not mean that its use by the Church is just a simple ceremony. It is a summons of the Church, charged with confidence; it carries the honor of a mission, the assurance of a special grace. It does not create the spiritual marriage, but it establishes the soul in a path which, if rightly understood, ought to lead to it.

Most of us are a little like the foolish virgins of the Gospel who lost their chance of entering into the marriage feast, not because they slept, (for so did the wise virgins), but because they did not understand that the honor of bearing a torch brought with it the duty of maintaining it. Therefore, we ought to consider the universal scope of St. Paul's words: "I have espoused you to one husband." Christ is to become Spouse to all? We see the Apostle perceiving it here as the final meaning of the Christian vocation; it follows then, that all the faithful are invited to the nuptials of the Lamb, and are bidden to love Christ even in this world with an exclusive and indissoluble love that should be constantly growing. What other purpose could the texts of the Constitutions on the Church and on the Liturgy have than to transform the relationship of Christians with Christ? In them the teaching of St. Paul regains its force through a more vital and more interior idea of the Church, and the term "spouse" simply represents the creature who, in the image of the divine Word, receives himself and gives himself completely according to the spirit.

St. Paul and St. Ignatius bear witness that holy men as well as holy women have longed for this fullness without excluding ardor and tenderness; and St. Bernard taught an unpolished army of monks what it meant for the soul to be spouse. St. John of the Cross did not believe that the spiritual marriage was reserved to his Carmelite daughters. Many practical men of action and many pontiffs have sung this nuptial song. Consider Pope John xxiii and the loving intimacy he reveals in his *Journal*.

If the spousal aspect of our relationship to Christ ought finally to prevail over every other, is it not in order to prefigure the heavenly state here on earth? Our Lord says that in heaven there will no longer be husband and wife in the human understanding of these words; in the regeneration, Christ will forever be the one and only Bridegroom. Without doing away with the beginnings of love realized by marriage in this world (for in all love there is something of the eternal), the relationships of this world will be transformed and absorbed into the sacrament of Christ and of the Church which is forever being consummated.

Those who will have preferred absolute love to every particular love "follow the Lamb wherever he goes" (Apoc 14, 4) and will follow him, therefore, in that effusion of glory and purity that will penetrate and transfigure every affection.

Would that all Christians could feel a presentiment of this transcendent joy so that, without leaving their earthly roads, every movement of their hearts could be directed toward their blessed life! The road has been prepared; life is given us in order that we may tend toward Christ the Spouse, and death that we may complete this perfect transformation. For when death is well understood, is it not the Christian leaving father and mother and land and house in order to go to Christ? Alone, and detached from everything, he has but to say "yes" in order to merit being presented to Christ "as a pure virgin."[2]

The scope of such a doctrine is truly immense, for it concerns all men. Yet, St. Paul's words suggest something still greater, for if Christ is the Bridegroom, he is involved in it himself; "as a partner" was said of the bride in Genesis (2, 18). The new Adam is not to be fulfilled by himself alone any more than the first one. He is called Jesus and so becomes himself only in becoming savior. Those who cause him to be savior, are those who let themselves be saved completely, who let themselves be made one with the love which he reveals in himself. Christ is not a center of attraction situated beyond and above us. He is eager to find himself; he seeks himself[3] when he seeks us; our supernatural life is a drama in which he is involved.

We have already seen something of the scope of this appeal and of what is at stake in this drama: "As the Father has loved me, so I have loved you." The import of Christ's action—and what we could call his vital need—is to reproduce in us, on the created level of grace, the relationship which unites him to his Father. It is essential that he restore everything to his Father. It is in this relationship of Bridegroom with his own that he intends to transmit to them all the love of the Father and to raise up to the Father all the love that is given to himself.

If spiritual marriage can be considered as uniting a soul to the divinity, it is because it is first of all union with Christ: "No one comes to the Father but by me" (Jn 14, 6). There is one thing we should note: when we speak here of a created union we are supposing that Christ is Bridegroom particularly according to his humanity. In fact, St. Teresa declares that the soul is introduced to the spiritual marriage through the intervention of this sacred humanity.[4]

Although the term "spiritual marriage" may seem reserved to mystical literature, the reality it represents is meant for every Christian. Its normal place is in the Eucharistic Sacrifice: the Mass is the sign and instrument of union with Christ. The sign, for it represents this union through the gift of his life and his Person which the Lord makes to us in the holy Sacrifice, and through Communion which joins our humanity with his. It is the instrument, for it builds this holy union through all it brings of purification and spiritual fervor and interior transformation, whose efficacy only we can limit.

"I have espoused you to one husband": there is here a promise of marriage which can and ought to be fulfilled in this life; there is also a nuptial institution: the Mass, in which the Lord Jesus is both Offering and Sacrifice. The spontaneous action of the Mass is a celebration, and every celebration is filled with his entire self; he is its minister, not from afar through some official act, but by the ardor of his heart and in total presence.

The desire of the Apostle and that of the Lord are satisfied when a soul understands that Jesus is whole and entire in his sacrificial act, and when it consents to meet him in it and not seek him elsewhere.

NOTES

1. VII, 1:3.
2. Knowing further that this "yes" does not perpetuate a definite break, but only the perfect order of love, which is so difficult to accomplish here on earth.
3. "He will save me in saving himself" (Blaise Pascal, *Mystery of Jesus*).
4. See VII, 2:1.

XXIX
At the Heart of the Church

We are used to looking upon the life of union with God as a private enterprise, which is offered through a special grace and pursued in the secret of one heart to another, and which results in a personal transformation.

In actual fact, the "spiritual marriage," which is the peak of the life of union, overflows the narrow borders of this ideal through its social aspect. Therefore, it takes on a significance that perhaps we consider too rarely.

Nevertheless, it is one of the summits of the Gospel. The great sacerdotal prayer of Christ contains two main ideas that are linked together: the Lord asks that his own be united to him as he is to the Father; and that they be united among themselves so as to make but one (see Jn 17, 21).

The first request corresponds exactly to the essence of spiritual marriage. The second expresses its social consequence. We can see that the importance that Jesus attaches to this is since it is the supreme point of his teaching.

We speak of social consequence because every marriage founds a family and by that fact more or less gives direction to society. In the same way, Jesus suggests in his last words to us that our union with him introduces into the world the life of the divine Family, with a unity that is its own proper perfection: "That all may be one as you, Father, are in me and I in you." In this way spiritual marriage guides history by its providential interpretation. In practice, we can see that spiritual marriage is needed first of all to *constitute* human society, and then to *preserve* it in its proper function.

Human society cannot be constituted by its own resources alone. We see clearly that, of itself, it seeks its meaning and its equilibrium in vain. It poses more problems than it resolves. It is more often a battlefield than a beneficial framework for life. By itself, society has no means for attaining true unity. The reason for this weakness is that the human marriage which founds it has lost its unifying power along with its spiritual efficacy.

Human marriage needs to be completed by the "spiritual marriage." Then Christ becomes the organic center of society, and society "holds together" in the measure in which each of its members holds to him, that is in the measure in which it is Christian. "I in them, and you in me—that they may become perfectly one" (Jn 17, 23). This is the great rule.

Since man needs to be born again in order to belong to Christ, the first function of marriage according to the spirit is to propagate divine life. Providence has reserved this fruitfulness especially to those who are consecrated to Christ. To be sure, this consecration is the final vocation for everyone, but for it to be perfect it must exclude, without exception, all other concerns.

Hence, there are two sources of life: one natural, the other supernatural. It is part of God's plan that they should not be confused; and the Church takes care to distinguish between them.

The primitive plan of marriage has been divided in order to be the better reestablished; the new Adam is henceforth solely responsible for transmitting life in the spiritual order. Would he leave those who are united to him on the margin of human development? The Lord still continues to say to all: "Be fruitful and multiply" (Gn 9, 1). Would the second of the two ministries be the less enriching?

By modifying a little the Pauline symbol of the two alliances, we could say that the one begets servitude, the other liberty. (see Gal 4, 22–27). Be that as it may, the two currents ought to converge and the two institutions collaborate—but not on the same level. St. Paul declares of marriage: "This is a great sacrament!" But he is careful to add: great "in Christ and in the Church" (Eph 5, 32, Douai). It is as if he said that human marriage would be without real greatness unless it were in harmony with the spiritual marriage that completes it. For the latter is really nothing else than the concrete realization in souls of the mystery of Christ and of the Church.

Actually, husband and wife are themselves urged by the grace of the sacrament to achieve their union in God, spiritually. If this appeal were answered truly, there would be perfect equilibrium in society. But, on the contrary, if the love that God demands from men does not come to full flower in and through human affections, it must be sought in concurrence with these affections. And this is a division (see 1 Cor 7, 33). As a matter of fact, society—even Christian society—scarcely goes beyond this concurrence. This is the reason equilibrium must be reestablished through special vocations, not only to assure the permanency of this society, but also to maintain its authentic Christian meaning.

This is the special role of those whom we designate as "consecrated" and "contemplative." How are these to react on social life? The answer seems easy: through prayer. Is the dynamism of these consecrated souls principally in the diligence of their intercession? The world thinks so, and indeed they do owe this assiduity to Christian society. Yet, they have a more essential duty than that of furnishing "prayers"; they must "be prayer." They are this in the measure in which they are spiritually virgins, that is, spouses of Christ on the level of the Seventh Mansions.

At this degree the virgin is truly virgin. She is a creature without earthly support, without human goal, without any other craving than Christ. She is wholly an appeal to the Lord which is of great value in his eyes. Picture the prayer of those holy ones of old—especially the mute longing of their misery. God understood it: "Your brother's blood is crying to me" (Gn 4, 10). To be capable of a hunger worthy of the spirit, not to cheat in regard to her profession of being poor or be disturbed by it, this is to be virgin as the Blessed Virgin was, and like her to be prayer.

But this goes far deeper than simply being a power in the Christian society we call the Church. The Blessed Virgin represents the Church. Following her, the virgin who is truly virgin expresses the Church concretely as a spouse.

The Church on earth, Virgin because she is Spouse, is completely a call to Jesus Christ. There is no doubt that she possesses him. Nevertheless, she also seeks him, because she has never finished being enlightened and assimilated by him.

When the communicant has received the Lord, he must turn himself toward his Lord or he will not really be a communicant. For Jesus will not "come" completely into a soul until he has wholly penetrated it forever. In like manner, the Church would become hardened and materialistic if she were restricted to possessing her Spouse. She would not then be Spouse according to the Spirit.

Actually, the Spirit inspires her with quite another attitude. In the Church as in souls, his sighs, too deep for words (see Rom 8, 26), are a call. St. John teaches this at the end of the Apocalypse where he sums up the plan of this divine guide in conducting us through the vicissitudes of the Church of earth: "The Spirit and the Bride say: Come" (Apoc 22, 17).

In this world Jesus is properly called "He who comes." It is the name St. John the Baptist used when he asked: "Are you he who is to come?" (Lk 7, 19–21) It is the name Jesus gives himself: "Surely I am coming soon" (Apoc 22, 20).

The Church says her "Come" through the sacraments she administers, through each of her consecrations, through her faith, through her apostolate. The special work of the Council is a stirring "Come."

Thus, riches and poverty mingle in the life of the Church: "As having nothing, and yet possessing all things" (2 Cor 6, 10). Along with the consciousness of her greatness, she must maintain an awareness of her needs. She is beautiful in the exercise of her power and beautiful also in her "Come," through which she is more able to permeate the world, especially those who seek her.

The Church must contain in herself, not only the structure of the hierarchy so that she may spread her treasures abroad, but also an element that can maintain the freshness of the humility and poverty that make her "Come" a living spring.

This element is spiritual virginity. Certainly there are holy Pastors who possess it, but it is especially her "consecrated" virgins who are called upon to be its faithful source in place of any other service. How important it is for them to be totally virgin through a total interior poverty! For what else is virginity but love under the protection of poverty?

Are such souls numerous? Without doubt, they are not. In the house of God the greater number of Christians are children rather than spouses; they are secure under the surveillance of their Mother the Church. When St. Paul feels it his duty to call them to higher things, he does so only with some precautions. His "I have espoused you" has a preamble which sounds anxious: "I wish you would bear with me in a little foolishness. Do bear with me. I feel a divine jealousy with you." This timid opening is much in line with the Master's: "He who is able to receive this [teaching] let him receive it" (Mt 19, 12).

Do we find some of these little children even among virgins who are proud of their title?

Few listen to or comprehend the divine jealousy. Very few

indeed carry their understanding of its appeal all the way to its real end. Yet, who can express the full efficaciousness of these few?

No doubt it is a hidden efficaciousness, even a simply corporate one; and yet, it is not unusual for it to become visible. When St. Teresa was dying and called herself a "daughter of the Church," was she only affirming her submission? In that hour of supreme fulfillment, may she not have had a humble but luminous perception of the connaturality between herself and the great mystical reality for which she had lived?

Perceptible to the heart and sometimes visible exteriorly; in some way this is normal. Is not one who is truly spouse in the home of the Bridegroom also mistress of the house by right? The wife is the life of the family; she initiates and directs the activities of the household; she sets the tone of its social life.

In like manner, those who are truly spouses of Christ are in the Church as animators of its life in many different ways. Considering only the field of interior works, we think at once of St. Teresa, "Spiritual Mistress," of St. Margaret Mary, of St. Therese of the Child Jesus, of Elisabeth of the Trinity and others, and of the ways of fervor and confidence and love that they have opened up. These quiet but penetrating currents circulate the substance of dogmas throughout the Church, making them easier to be assimilated.

In this way, the active life is impregnated with contemplative values; it is vitalized by them. These souls who have lived in God's country spread abroad his vigor, all the while keeping for themselves his incommunicable secret. This kind of efficacy is a superabundance.

Let us return to the essential point. Even though it is entirely within the realm of being, perfect virginity can be hidden and seem socially inefficacious. But does the appearance matter? Being which is fully alive is completely one with its interior act; its life may be overlooked by many, but it manifests itself unrestrainably. It is like a pocket of water under desert sand; we do not see it, but we deduce its presence from the oasis it produces.

This quality of being, as well as the act which springs spontaneously from it, is the only sure source of the lived Gospel. Silently it presents to those around it, and then to all the world, the doctrine of Jesus in a perpetual renewal. It spreads abroad his spirit. It is the necessary climate for genuine prayer "in the name of Jesus," because it makes the soul adhere to Christ and frees it from all other dependence.

No doubt many do not reach the point of "spiritual marriage"; nevertheless, they are not useless. How many blossoms fall before giving any fruit! Yet, we are grateful to them for being there as a sign of spring. The Church, however, wants her summer. She needs fruitful blossoms.

"All my life I live in thee," was St. Teresa's song.[1] The dart of the seraphim not only entered into the very center of her being, but came out again, pulling and drawing out this center with it, so that her life was no longer contained in herself and measured by "self." She received a new dimension, the total supernatural dimension.

St. Teresa is referring to this dimension when she says: "I could no longer desire anything but God."[2] But she expresses it especially in becoming herself an effusion of love. In so doing, she proves the intimate relationship between spiritual maternity and virginity, when this latter has arrived at its perfection. Did not Jesus tell us this himself? "Whoever drinks of the water that I shall give him will never thirst"; and again: it "will become in him a spring of water, welling up to eternal life" (Jn 4, 13–14).

Thus, we are shown that, when life is truly Christian, it does not end within us. It is fullness, but it is also fruitfulness which comes about spontaneously and ordinarily through the simple fact that it is a *real* participation in the life of Christ. It is this *real* union which is meant when we say: "to believe in Jesus"; "to drink of his water." We mean a total faith through which a soul no longer takes support in what it sees and experiences, but rests completely in its Savior. We mean it so finds its happiness in him—in his doctrine, his gifts, and his promises—that the thirst of its entire being is quenched and it forgets the childish thirsts for "self" which dry up the flow of water.

Then a soul is mysteriously established "in the heart of the Church" in the power of the Spirit of Jesus. This is what the Gospel says. It is not a function reserved for a few, but is offered to all. Are we living springs in Christian society? Everything depends on our will for accomplishment. If we stop half-way, is it because we are not able, or because we do not want to go the whole way to the end of the road?

Rather, it is chiefly because we neglect the initial steps: We do not understand the First Mansions properly; we disdain to live the Second to the full; mistakenly we settle ourselves down in the Third; we do not use the advances of the Fourth to advantage; thus, we do not arrive at the Fifth which hold the key to true life.

What the symbol of the Mansions expresses is the significance of sin, of virtuous effort, of grace, and most of all of charity in the life of a child of God. Let us make the effort to examine our mediocrities and our reservations in the light of these great realities.

NOTES

1. *Poems*, II.
2. *Life*, XXIX.

SOME PRACTICAL
REFLECTIONS

XXX
True and False Supports

Are there any signs by which we can tell if we are becoming contemplatives? Contemplation may be a mystery, because its divine Object is invisible, but it is not a fact that cannot be verified. There are some landmarks: objects which have been left behind. The traveler does not judge the speed of an express train directly; he ascertains it by watching the trees and houses disappear behind him.

In the landscape of the human goods over which we have to travel, do our needs, our desires, and especially our honor stand before us like fixed objects to which our interest is attached? Or are they like fleeting mirages that quickly fade from view? The speeding course which bears the soul away from itself is the practice of the interior "election": that spontaneous choice of God at all times in the depths of the soul which is fundamental for contemplation. Choosing God means choosing humble and never-ending virtue; it means choosing the authority he delegates and adhering to it with the heart of a child.

But how do we put all this into practice? What do we do when we come to the practical level? Sometimes we overlook the deep, clear reality of contemplative life that we have been considering in these many chapters, and base our spiritual life on supports which are good in themselves, but inadequate for sustaining us on so arduous a journey. We can let ourselves be captivated by formulas of spirituality, for we like to know where we are going and a formula seems to answer this need. Because the road of the interior life is ordinarily obscure, those who travel it are apt to have a liking for word-programs and well-defined itineraries, like maps in color.

There is an inevitable discrepancy between the spiritual reality and the idea that we form of it when it is put into words. Words have their magic; they also bear the risk of being just words. Doctrines are necessary; but if they are insufficiently assimilated, they can lead to a kind of nominalism, which is not the road to the contemplative election.

What is needed is a virtue that we may not think of cultivating enough: the virtue of understanding[1]; it is fundamental. "Because they do not regard the works of the Lord," says the psalmist, "he will break them down and build them up no more" (Ps 28, 5). Likewise, we read in the Book of Wisdom that the Holy Spirit withdraws himself from thoughts that are without understanding (see Wis 1, 5).

Such understanding is not the result of a keen intellect; rather, it is a sense of the real in the supernatural order. To understand this better, consider the words of the author of Wisdom: "In her, (Wisdom), there is a spirit, intelligent, holy unique, manifold, subtle, mobile, clear, unstained, distinct, invulnerable, loving the good, keen, irresistible, beneficent, humane, steadfast, secure, free from anxiety, all-powerful, overseeing all, and penetrating through all spirits that are intelligent and pure and most subtle" (Wis 7, 22–23).

What strikes us first in this enumeration is an apparent disorder. Yet, a more methodical arrangement might show less clearly the extent to which these aspects are tied together; they are like the facets of a diamond, varied incidences of light, one single light whose reflections are multipled. In the *Interior Castle*, the diamond is the image of the soul, and the text we have just quoted forms part of the liturgical office of St. Teresa. Thus, we can consider these different aspects of the "spirit of understanding" as blessings which the Saint desires for her followers and which mark spiritual progress.

The first thing we see is that this "spirit of understanding" is closely connected with the heart. It is sweet, "loving the good, beneficent, kindly, tranquil."

This is reassuring to those who fear intellectualism whenever intelligence is mentioned. They want nothing but love. Who would blame them? But here intelligence is presented as tied to love. There is no danger of intellectualism in that; rather, there is much more danger in the oversimplification of formulas. Why? Because although the formula aims at the heart, it is addressed to the mind. It does not go straight to the goal—the center of the will. Understanding that is according to God reaches this center; the will is perfected in exact proportion to its relationship with the understanding. This is what makes it free, for liberty is adhesion in actual practice to the divine plan, and understanding is the witness to this plan.

It is not only the witness, but the instrument. The formula is approximate; it can only suggest. "The spirit of understanding," as the sacred author tells us, is keen and subtle.

Nature has provided animals with an extraordinarily exact sense for distinguishing what is suited to them and for knowing how to obtain it. Why should God not offer his children some means of investigation as keen as the dog's sense of smell, and a sense of orientation as fine as that which the swallow possesses?

To be able to act, that is, to be able to fulfill our election at every moment with ease and perfection, we need an instinct. Our spiritual security is rather pitiful if its only support is a picture of the goal it is to attain and a calculation of the means. St. Paul wants us to desire the security of "God's own peace, which passes all understanding" (Phil 4, 7). It passes beyond all reasoned and perceptible ways of conduct because it is the working of divine instinct.

St. John affirms this: "We know that the Son of God has come and has given us understanding" (1 Jn 5, 20). This sure sense of the things of God communicates a great steadfastness, which we practice in the discernment of values, as essential function. The "Spirit of understanding" teaches and directs without equivocation. On the practical level it is a perspicacity which says: "No!"

There are some "yeses" that we are almost compelled to say "yes" to the whims of the imagination and the caprices of nature; "yes" to flattering influences, whatever be our milieu; "yes" to alluring theories, to superficial points of view, to polished formulas.

The "no" of the understanding is a demand for genuine value, the protest of life in depth against superficial activities on the surface. Moreover, usually the refusal will not be complete, because there is some good in what tempts us. But this half-good is not enough for true life. Only a holy understanding can tell us what we need for that, for it is the only faculty over which appearances have no hold.

It is, therefore, an organ which discerns in depth: its power of refusal is primordial, at the root of the election, and, consequently, of the contemplative life where half-goods wage an incessant offensive in thousands of ways.

Note well that this refusal is not to be confused with the refusal of the will. The "no" of the understanding is an instinctive reaction that precedes all decision. It puts the judgment on guard against what does not come from above by "confounding the waves" whose origin is too human. Or, using another comparison, it is not a switch that is operated at will, but a circuit breaker that automatically shuts off the currents that do not lead to God.

Lack of understanding, perhaps more than lack of generosity, causes many souls—although in love with the contemplative life—to get bogged down on the way without even realizing it, so that, in spite of their more-or-less satisfactory effort, they do not arrive at the goal. Full of piety, of merit, and of human prudence, they do not discover the one precious pearl for which they must leave all.

No matter how frequent this lapse may be, it is not irremediable. Understanding, considered from God's point of view, is not what we call understanding in the human domain: a limited gift, measured and reserved. St. John affirms that an instinctive sense of divine things is given by the Son of God and is received through the power of Baptism, being strengthened in the sacrament of Confirmation. Nevertheless, we must put this magnificent talent to good use, for if we do not make it our own, it may remain unproductive. For this reason we have spoken of the *virtue* of understanding, which must be exercised in conjunction with the gift of God.

The chief thing is to start on the road by means of a forceful decision: "I prayed and understanding was given me" (Wis 7, 7). This indicates the prayer of petition, but conditioned by a vigorous "choice." The rest of the text shows this clearly enough: "I preferred her (Wisdom) to scepters and thrones, and I accounted wealth as nothing in comparison with her, neither did I liken to her any priceless gem; because all gold is but a little sand in her sight, and silver will be accounted as clay before her. I loved her more than health and beauty and I chose to have her rather than light" (Wis 7, 7–10).

In a word, our choice entails sacrifice and contempt for everything that counts in men's eyes. Without this immense and costly act, any pretension to holy understanding is vain. We must train ourselves in this.

This is exactly what St. Teresa proposes. The assignment she gives us to "to dig until we find."[2] To dig, that is, through repeated efforts to make progress toward depth. Without respite until we find, because there is no vacation from contemplative work.

By digging down, the spirit to some extent renounces the light. This is the critical point at which we often draw back, for here we must refuse to seek rest in ideas which are on our own level, and must know how to escape from the gilded cage of clear perceptions[3]; this is a liberation that is not achieved without anxiety. But, like every virtue, the virtue of understanding is a strength, and consists precisely in walking without flinching through this apparent void.

This should not be confused with a taste (somewhat uncommon) for the obscure and the indefinite, which may be provoked by an inadequate reading of certain mystics. The work of deepening produces a great poverty of spirit. It is choice fulfilled, but we have still to receive its fruit.

The spirit is filled to the brim in its poverty by a maturing which is the work of supernatural understanding. We might call it "the sense of being," for its essence is discerning what has the value of being and adhering to it. At this point, the refusals become powerful; it is also by dint of saying "no" and of digging deep that the spirit of understanding, "which nothing hinders," no longer knows any obstacle and finds its very self in encountering its divine Object.

Whence can this sense of being actually come except from contact with Him who Is? For all that, we must not think of the contact as something reserved to a few. St. Paul writes to the Ephesians: "Look carefully how you walk"; and then continues: "Be filled with the Spirit" (Eph 5, 15–18). He seeks the effect in its true cause. It is not a wish, but a command. We are not aware how true it is that our Lord is waiting at the door, ready to fill everything.

Why are souls closed to him? The sacred text again provides the answer: the spirit of understanding is "pure, holy, unstained"; "nothing that is sullied enters into it."

Many may retain certain subconscious, camouflaged weaknesses; an inability to mortify the heart of self-love; a resentment; a bit of jealousy; of conceit; of ambition; human opinions; an honesty of behavior that is too relative; a superficiality that makes very interior purifications impossible. Many weaknesses of this kind keep at the threshold the Spirit who would like to invade us totally but cannot, because he has a horror not only of sin, but of malfunctions of the will.[4]

The understanding that comes from the Spirit penetrates to the depths of virtue, depths it needs in order to rest therein.

The interior life vegetates when the sure and pliant life of the intellect is lacking, for as Scripture says, Wisdom is the source of that life both in its essence and in its fruits: "She makes friends of God and prophets" (Wis 7, 27). What is apt to happen then is that the will discovers an aid that we call the "good intention," and which can be deceptive.

"I want what is good, therefore, my intentions are good, my faults are involuntary and can do me no harm." We say this to ourselves sometimes, and thus find security for living piously sheltered from agitation and spiritual anxiety.

How much is this support worth? With all due respect to many, perhaps what is most lacking in such an understanding of the "good intention" is the intention—simply just that.

The intention, as the word suggests, is a movement directed with precision and vigor toward its object. Precision is lacking if we love the good only in general. If our resolve for perfection springs only from feeling, our action will be weak. These are good dispositions, but not genuine intention.

Is it astonishing that a multitude of imperfections may pass unseen through such an open mesh? Doubtless, we do not will the imperfection, but not to will a fault expressly is not sufficient to make us not responsible for it. We must tend toward the good with a real intention which abhors "almosts" and every avoidable weakness.

This natural requirement is fundamental. What must we think about the "good intention" when we consider it in its supernatural sense? We could say that it is the dynamism of charity, or rather, the preparation of the potential of charity that a soul possesses.

There are two elements: using monetary terms, the first is like a principal, a capital, which is both acquired and received and which is not subject to improvisation. Does it not sometimes happen that we look upon the good intention as a simple expedient of which the will is capable at any moment? From this comes our idea of the act of perfect charity. It is taken for granted that we shall produce it to merit a plenary indulgence and again at the hour of death.

Primarily, however, the quality and dimension of this act are in proportion to the charity that is in the soul: "Love is the measure of my worth." We have to realize that the good intention is a fortune to be gained, a power to be formed. A right understanding of this, deep in the soul, is something we must seek and pray for: "Create in me a clean heart, O Lord, and put a new and right spirit within me" (Ps 51, 10). Then it becomes easier to acknowledge oneself at fault even in regard to the intention. This means renouncing every false aid and entering reality.

It does not mean resigning oneself to chronic imperfection. The value of the intention can always increase. It grows through its second element. No matter how poor our charity may be, if it is continually tending toward making itself real— that is toward governing our every step—then it achieves victory. Then our "capital" bears fruit and obtains perpetual increase from God.

Furthermore, our personal effort is not to be understood as an effort of intensity, but as an effort of purity. Only God stirs up our ardor. To some he gives more, to others less. But each soul has as much holy understanding as it desires: "I prayed and understanding was given to me"; it is the vital center of the good intention.[5] When its exercise is understood in this way, it has a power without limit: "In your glory and majesty, ride forth victoriously" (Ps 45, 4)—such is the chain reaction promised by the Holy Spirit.

He is also the only witness of this disposition. "The Spirit himself," writes St. Paul, "bears witness with our spirit—that we are children of God" (Rom 8, 16); in other words, that we are acting in charity.

Can we conclude that we find true support here, an incontestable verification? Yes, but at the same time let us be aware of how the Holy Spirit gives testimony. It is not ordinarily through sensible signs. He is not given to us as a spiritual pressure gauge to measure the pressure in numerical figures.

The very fact that a soul is tending to the service of God above all is in itself the testimony of the Holy Spirit. It is his testimony because it is his own work. Observe that this tending can have nothing triumphal about it. But if it persists, if it continues steadfastly to inspire practical decisions, then it is a voice which cries, "Abba," in the Holy Spirit. It becomes like second nature. It maintains the life of the good intention. Thus, there is formed in the soul what we could call the "sense of purpose."

We see that "false supports" are opposed by two sustaining forces, but how mysterious they are, and how difficult to conquer: the sense of being; the sense of purpose.

Are these disappointing conclusions? God forbid! True, the supports offered bear little resemblance to the ground we like to feel beneath our feet. They are more like wings which invite us to fly. Is that a state of equilibrium? Most certainly it is, for as the psalmist sings, uniting both ideas: "O that I had wings like a dove, I would fly away and be at rest" (Ps 55, 6).

Let us acknowledge once again that a holy objectivity is our entire good, and understand how this kind of support is suited to this good, since the characteristic of the truly supernatural life is to find its equilibrium in its movement beyond itself. It is normal for us to be "aliens and exiles" (1 Pt 2, 11) on this earth; we must be the same in our interior act.

In Jesus and his Gospel of poverty, we see the perfect support: "Blest are you poor; for yours is the kingdom of God" (Lk 6, 20). He who ceaselessly shakes off the weight of things and of himself, he it is who adheres to being, who runs to this goal, who is nourished with holy understanding.

NOTES

1. The "virtue" of understanding: the phrase may seem unusual. It has reference to the whole practical and voluntary context in which the gift of understanding is displayed: preparations, reception, utilization. It would seek to avoid the too purely theoretical and gratuitous aspect which the idea of understanding in the interior life sometimes has in our eyes.
2. v, 1:2, Peers.
3. It is necessary to distrust what seems clear through habit—clichés of spirituality, and easy views which please the imagination—for what is sensible is closer to matter than to the spirit. Feeling must tend toward giving way rather than to satisfying itself. In the measure in which feeling thus withdraws, understanding loses its perceptible support and becomes obscure. At the same time, however, it no longer diverts the spirit and becomes more directly the *mover*.
4. "Wisdom will not enter a deceitful soul" (Wis 1,4).
5. The understanding is the center of the good intention: understanding is expressed and concluded, not in itself, but in the will's election. Are not those things which seem to us characteristic of the intellect—intellectual representation

and images—only a temporary part of its road? In heaven we shall see that true light has its source in the act of love. May not the nights of earth be the intellect's progress beyond secondary functions toward its essential vocation?

XXXI
The Direct Road—In Principle

If there are weak and uncertain methods for entering into the reality of the contemplative life, there are also simple ways which go straight to the goal. St. Teresa sums up her doctrine clearly when she says in the *Way of Perfection:* "We must learn to cross our will in everything; although we may not succeed at once, yet little by little ... without knowing how, we shall reach the summit of perfection."[1]

We are well aware that, for her, "perfection" is something quite different from a collection of unshakeable virtues: it is simplicity of heart in charity. Hence, it is spiritual understanding with all the qualities enumerated in the Book of Wisdom and considered in the previous chapter. It is the intention, ever active in full objectivity. In a word, it is the complete vitality of the sense of being and of the sense of purpose.

The Saint assures us that there is a way to reach this summit without a profusion of mystical graces. To reach? No, rather to find oneself there, without tension, fatigue, or precise calculations: "little by little," she says, "without knowing how."

We will attempt to discern this way by answering several questions: What does "crossing our will" mean? Why is it a privileged way? How can we carry out this program?

"Crossing our will" is not a counsel to extreme asceticism. It is not a matter of stifling every outbreak of autonomy. Rather, it means disengaging our power of action from the false dynamism of the passions. When "passions" are mentioned, we are apt to picture the excesses and violent impulses which some temperaments have in certain situations. We scarcely suppose them present in a virtuous and well-regulated life.

Now, every life is more or less warped by the passions. We are slaves without knowing it. Our judgments, our decisions, the better part of ourselves, are governed by instincts, that is, by tendencies that are not directed by a completely pure and disinterested intention.

The will that we are talking about crossing is that spontaneity which we are inclined to see as being innocent; and ordinarily it is innocent; but, without our being conscious of the fact, it is animated by human motivations as well as by "good sentiments." We are saying to "cross," not to destroy. What does it mean to cross? First of all, it means not being the dupe of "self," and admitting the necessity of control. Then, it means exercising this control, by not giving unlimited authority to the movements of heart and fancy. Like a flock of sheep that have to be counted and sorted out, we have to restrain our impulses when we come to the narrow gate, so that our "sheep" may pass through it one by one and be recognized.

Finally, to cross means not only to use self-control, but to "contradict," that is, to say the contrary. Since, under cover of a "good intention," our will instinctively tends to satisfy nature and to favor its liberty, we have to contradict this will by supernatural objectivity.

Our plan must be untiringly to upset plans that are consciously or unconsciously too human, and to quell our reflex movements in "everything" (ordinarily through very small acts). You will say: everybody knows this; it is the rule of mortification, a cliché in spirituality. But do we know it in a practical way? It may help us to understand St. Teresa, to see why this exercise is so necessary.

It is necessary, first of all, on the natural plane. We do not acquire solid balance without some constraint; the error of too idealistic ways of education is the belief that it is enough to show some one the good and make it appreciated, in order to bring about a genuine pursuit of righteousness. Moral good can be obtained only by going against the current of our instincts, even when the question seems insignificant. In addition, we have violent instincts, such as those of domination, conceit, and independence, which an indirect approach will not suffice to appease. These must be dominated step by step, at any price, or at least be made to follow each fall with due reparation under pain of our being forced to endure their unrestrained tyranny. Our powers of inhibition become paralyzed when they have no exercise. We can even arrive at the point of being helpless before the last repugnance or natural impatience.

How will a person as weak as this be able to yield himself to the workings of grace? Even his judgment is not free. Everything in him is subjective; he lives in an atmosphere of sin without knowing it. No one has the right to judge another's responsibilities, but the sway of such a man's undominated reflexes is a plain fact.

This state can coexist, even in an intense degree, with pretensions to an interior life. The worst is not this extreme paradox, which is exceptional enough, but the fact that it is not rare to find a more benign form in lives which consider themselves virtuous, nay, even contemplative.

We need well-regulated faculties and subordinated passions for choosing the good in a way that is both effective and coherent. Nothing can take the place of this elementary order. Hence, Christian and religious training must necessarily begin and continue for a long time on this natural level.

It is less urgent to incite souls to generosity and to very elevated views than it is to attend closely to the objectivity of the judgment, to the sources of affectivity, to the control of choices. How often we speak of interior trials and aridities when we ought to be paying heed to childish indolence, an artificial use of talents, superficial tendencies.

Cutting out everything false, calling mediocrity by its name, and making very human causes understood is not the easiest kind of formation to give or to receive. Yet, how many failures in the spiritual life or in moral conduct could be avoided if impulses were gently disciplined with an untiring clear-sightedness and care. Now, what does contradicting and re-straining and rectifying our instinctive demands really mean, if not "to cross our [natural] will"?

The life of grace is implied in this rectification. It exacts something more than natural balance; it lives by a constant movement of contradiction. Why? Because charity cannot be sustained in us in the same way as in God. God is "love" as necessarily as he *is*! "God is love" (1 Jn 4, 8); "I am who am" (Ex 3, 14). But we are not necessarily tied either to being or to the essential Object of our love. With regard to being, we are only a contingency; with regard to the Object, we are ambiguous. Only when we have made a perfect election with our whole will, will this ambiguity cease. Then we shall have re-sponded to grace and shall have entirely entered into true life.

For this to come about, it is not enough for us to have a good heart and a beautiful ideal, just as it is not enough for a locomo-tive to have a good engine and a good engineer. A good switch-ing system is also necessary. For the train to cross over several tracks and come out on the right one, all but the right one have to be blocked. Crossing our will means, in a supernatural sense, blocking off the roads that do not lead straight to our divine End.

Because these crossroads open up by themselves, it is neces-sary, even in the state of innocence, for us to say "no" to self in order to have the opportunity to say a real *yes* to God. It is a question of proper switching.

This is an easy thing for a healthy creature to do. An interior movement is enough to assure the right direction, just as a light touch moves a well-regulated mechanism. No doubt this is the reason why the first act of self-denial that was proposed to man was something quite harmless in its material aspect. Since the Fall, however, nature is a tool that has been forced. It is difficult to work with. It needs the grasp of a divine hand and the lever of the cross. The cross is not redemptive only in the sense that it repairs the past. It would be of little use to have our innocence restored to us if we were simply put back in the ambiguous position our first parents had not known how to face. Christ supplies the remedy for this hazard by urging the Christian to follow him on the road of the cross. Through baptism we are crucified and buried with him; through the Mass we announce his death; through Communion we participate in him.

However it may seem, there is a positive orientation in this, a switching system. We enter the proper track by "crossing our will." Nothing can supplant the efficacy of this act. Neither can anything hinder it from producing its effect. The train, diverted from the wrong tracks, rolls along on the right one all the way to the end. The soul that contradicts its natural bent will finish on the "summit of perfection" without having to search out other secrets.

Because we do not grasp this principle, we run the risk of being fooled by imitations. Many souls think themselves in love with perfection and given over to God and yet make no progress in real love. They do not wrench themselves away from unworthy pursuits, or from indulging in sensitiveness and touchiness. This is not the reign of Jesus.

The switching system has not been working. They have been contented with accomplishments that are childish, exterior, in word only. The arrow of sacrifice must pierce the most secret regions of the heart. If these secret barriers will not let themselves be penetrated, if we are too skillful in repairing the

breeches, ambiguity subsists and the God of love does not enter. The result is mediocrity.

False perspectives as well as a more-or-less conscious aspiration for personal excellence can insinuate themselves even into
our desire for sanctity. These are shadows that cloud the
spiritual atmosphere.

Exactly what does it mean to be holy? It means to be *set apart
for God*. This is the Old Testament meaning; the first Christians
were called "saints" in the same sense of the word. If another
aspect, a "moral," sometimes banal, one has prevailed, may it
not be the result of a tendency to reduce everything to our
human measure? The primitive viewpoint is infinitely more
radical: To be separated for God is especially to be *separated
from oneself*.

Read the Gospel: Our Lord does not propose that we become
masterpieces of humanity, but, after his own example, to be
wholly dedicated souls who are scarcely concerned with themselves.

Does he even use the word "sanctity"? Yes, once at least, and
then in its complete sense: "Father," he says after the Supper,
"for them do I sanctify myself" (Jn 17, 19 Douai).[2] What does he
mean? The tragedy of the hour is a sufficient commentary. He
means: "For them, I am putting the finishing touch to losing
myself."

He still lives this mystery of "sanctity" on earth: he is the
holy Thing upon the altar which lets itself be forgotten, which
is present only in order to give itself—the Blessed Sacrament.
Of all that he is, he lets only his prodigality become visible for
the service of his Father and of his own.

Through this silent appeal, Jesus wishes to save us from ourselves and from our misconceptions. He holds out his hand for
love so that he can make it live its true life.

To be a Christian and to live in this essentially spiritual action ought to be one and the same thing. In actual fact, we are

hardly Christian. This is the reason why life "in the spirit" lacks witnesses; volunteers are needed to reveal it to the world.

NOTES

1. *Way of Perfection*, xii;3.
2. The R.S.V. and Jerusalem Bible say "consecrate" instead of "sanctify," the latter with the note that "consecrate" means to "sanctify" in the original sense of the word.

XXXII
The Direct Road—In Practice

Every contradiction, accepted as such in the name of the Lord, advances the work of which we are speaking. This is one of the points that distinguish truly Christian life from mere human undertakings: success and setback do not have the same meaning for both.

St. Teresa aimed high when, in drawing up Constitutions for her nuns, she demanded exact fidelity; a "rule of life" contributes to the same high goal for earnest Christians. The restraint that a rule of life imposes engages the will in a submission which is a concentration of energy and definitively keeps it for God.[1]

In fact, if we look carefully, we can see that even in a trifling contradiction, there is an element of great psychological value: the discipline of the passions. Nothing serious can be accomplished in the moral order unless the subconscious impetuosity of our impulses is reduced, for at the root of every instinctive movement lies egoism, the radical enemy of life according to the spirit.

How do we uncover its presence? "Self" has its enthusiasms which may often seem beneficial, and this fervor of the "flesh" (taking "flesh" in the Pauline sense of the word) can be naively confused with that of the "spirit."

Our passions are hidden and well camouflaged. It is a rather childish pretension to want to discover them and to insist on

recognizing them before combatting them. Teresa does not call
for such a study. From the first, by means of humble practices,
she engages us in action, in an action which may seem dispro-
portioned to the elevated existence she wants us to have, yet an
action of guaranteed efficacy.

The saints understood it in this way. "There is only one thing
to do," was Therese of Lisieux's bold assertion, "to offer our
Lord the flowers of little sacrifices."[2] Mark well, this was the
way in which she was aiming at the "summit of perfection."

By whatever means the soul rises up against its own instincts, it defends its liberty, frees its personality, and, what is
much more, puts itself on the level of grace. Thus, the psalmist
sings: "in the day of my trouble I seek the Lord, in the night my
hand is stretched out without wearying" (Ps 77, 2).

He sought God. How? In delights and enthusiasms? By sheer
force of will? In none of these ways, but in contradictions and
uncertitude, through humble actions and, in addition, by night,
without seeing how his work was going to reach its end.

Today some are trying to make the contemplative life more
approachable, to minimize its difficulties, and to create a kind
of spiritual humanism, thanks to which, it seems, Christians
could slip into union with God without trouble, and without
going beyond their natural sphere.

St. Teresa is not of this school. If there is a way to arrive at the
goal "little by little and without knowing how," it is, according
to her, through "crossing our wills in everything." She does not
know of any process of aclimatization that may evade this. God
takes it upon himself to provide the occasions: painful and
unforeseen happenings which wound our heart, our judgment,
our honor, our personal rights.

Since the characteristic of these trials is their being *submitted to,* we may wonder what they have to do with the wholly
voluntary decision we are discussing. It is true that ordinarily
we can think of no better way of responding to these trials than
with what we call patience. Yet, even in such a response there

is a kind of semifailure with regard to charity. "Patience" can be a poor thing, at least the attitude that we sometimes designate by this name and wrap ourselves in! Exteriorly we are restrained, but within, the heart remains disturbed. If suffering is a call of love, this is not the proper response, and St. John of the Cross is right when he says that souls rarely know how to make the decisive act which will permit the divine appeal to obtain the answer it is looking for.[3]

Consider again St. Therese's instruction, which is so authoritative beneath the honey of its words: "There is only one thing to do here below—to offer our Lord the flowers of little sacrifices."[4]

"Only one thing to do." This is something beyond theories of spirituality; rather, it is an act which sums up these theories and is their culmination. Is not our refusal to "lose ourself" the only real obstacle to the divine action? We have been looking for the psychological point where being sums itself up and surrenders itself in order to offer itself to the divine encounter; here we have found our doctor. Little sacrifices—their size is of no importance—these are the possibilities offered us at each moment to make the objectivity we are seeking actual.

There is "only one thing to do." The rather thorny flowers which Providence entrusts to us are not to be kept in a basket tied with purple ribbons, just to be looked at: St. Therese wants us to throw them to Jesus—she herself liked to toss them very high.

This is the proper act and the fruitful reply to the hour of agonizing appeal. We must "throw" to Jesus what he claims from those who are his, even though he may use our neighbor as his unconscious intermediary. It is the most intense, the most efficacious act of which we are then capable. Jesus himself teaches this royal use of liberty at the hour when the heart *submits* and chooses to be without defenses: "No one takes [my life] from me, but I lay it down of my own accord" (Jn 10, 18).

"My life" . . . this is truly the essential question, for whether the matter of the trial be great or small, we are, by hypothesis, in the realm of the most intimate and essential values, which is the reason "little sacrifices" have such a special character when they go as far as this. Now, we have to take all this upon ourselves fully; St. Therese tells us so in a few words: "We must win him by our caresses."

What else is our "caress" than the sacrifice of what we call individuality? To accept not being, to turn ourselves completely toward him who is, this is the "caress" of the creature for his creator. To be willing to be a lost thing, to give free play to him who saves, is not this to "win Jesus" by a "caress" proportioned to him?

This is the unique moment—imperceptible perhaps, but supreme in quality—in which the Christian life bears its fruit of objectivity. For let us not fancy that our heart is capable of surrendering itself to God, really and definitively, without this providential pressure. In heaven, in the image of the Redeemer, all those who have conquered will bear the marks of his wounds; this is the reason we can associate without paradox what is least chosen in our lives with the decision that is most free and most magnificent.

"To take care" to cross our will is precisely to bring the total intimacy of acquiescence to bear upon the most deeply disconcerting provocation. There is a secret of achievement in this for every Christian, and much more for every religious. Indeed, we can say that acquiescence compels fulfillment like a river which loses itself in the sea. Neither observances nor vows, nor the most beautiful virtues, have any real meaning as long as they do not empty themselves into the mysterious estuary where at last they accept existence only for God.

Opportunities are not lacking, but the great temptation of our hearts is to attempt to escape from them. We are afraid of letting the best of ourselves be devalued. Yet, what we call personality is only a rind. The precious treasure, the "person," comes to light when the rind is removed. This is what St. Teresa means when she promises the "summit of perfection" as the reward of a radical contradiction.

We must fear the absurdity of a Christian life which operates only through secondary values. Then, it is not only an incomplete work but, according to the psalmist, *iniquity* (the fact of not being on our proper level) may lead to hatred[5]; this is equivalent to saying that, in the domain of charity, every insufficiency is a beginning of refusal.

God is not terrible in his demands, but nothing can keep love from being love; that is, nothing can keep it from being an essential activity, so that every accepted inertia is a slap in its face. Yet, our natural avarice constantly supports this inertia; and unless the soul uses an energy more obstinate than the resistance, it makes itself an accomplice of the obscure "no," which ceases then to be entirely involuntary.

It makes little difference whether the matter of the trial be great or small. To demand that we count "little trials" as nothing is not always even fair. It can be inhuman. Big or little, they must be completely accepted. We deceive souls, if, through compassion or what we call "comprehension," we let them believe that they can exempt themselves from this duty.

This is a harsh school, you will say. If the reality of the Christian life has to be bought so dearly, how can Jesus tell us that his yoke is easy and his burden light (see Mat 11, 29-30)? But notice that our Lord says first: "Take my yoke upon you," and only afterwards discloses that his yoke is easy. The strong action must precede; then the work of contradicting self tends to become plenitude and harmony.

Our supernatural will finds it a wearisome thing to feel itself always in arrears. Nature bounds ahead on every occasion; it is hard work to confront it, since it is filled with impetuosity. But the more this loving will gives itself up to the decisive affirmations mentioned above, the more it gains in depth and spontaneity of power. In consequence, the natural impulses become submissive in advance, as it were, captured at their source and impregnated with the supernatural from their very first effort, like the waters of Jericho which the prophet Elisha made healthy by purifying them at the place of their origin (see 2 Kgs 2, 21).

When we make use of this power, we are still contradicting self, for it leads nature where nature of itself would not want to go. However, this is no longer a combat, but a victory. "He who rises early to seek her will have no difficulty," is said of divine Wisdom (Wis 6:14). Is not this early morning quest the privilege of an already victorious love? It is fit and well, it is alert, it arises with joy while "nature" is still sleeping; the objections will come too late; they will be a proof rather than a danger.

We discover more than an ascetical recipe at the heart of Teresa's aggressive counsel: there is an initiation into the ways of love. The initiation is an indispensable one, for we are all like children in the great contest in which the Lord is pleased to engage with his creatures.

Whether the divine advances make us happy or whether they try us, their one purpose is to provoke an interior action. In order to acquire the sense and taste for such an action, we have to say no to the false need of possession and the false instinct of self-preservation. This is what St. Teresa calls "crossing our will." This "no," which at first is an effort and then becomes a power, is the work of the Fifth and Sixth Mansions; it is the secret of the Seventh. It puts a soul on the level of the divine Partner; for when we forget the matter of an act and its repercussions on the senses in order to live the act in itself, we are living by the ways of the spirit and are on the direct road toward an encounter with the Lord.

Is he not himself the truth that sets us free? Those who are his, true children of the Church, walk by a way which, despite

its shadows, is infallible in its origin and in its end. Their
security is born of faith, when faith is given its true dimensions
by love. It is the fruit of adoration "in spirit and in truth."

May Teresa of Avila reveal the secret to many! Is it too daring
to propose her as guide? Rather, is not such audacity one with
that of the Council which calls us all to the perfection of Love?

Doubtless it is not given to everyone to achieve this perfect
adoration, but we all need to seek it. The People of God on earth
is the seed of the Church of heaven. Its greatness lies in being a
living seed.

NOTES

1. Our age, in love with spontaneity, looks unfavorably on
   practices relating to self-control or to distrust of natural impulses. A certain moral impotence and delusion seem to be
   the consequence of this disdain. It would seem that a renewal might be proposed under the title, "revision of life."
2. *Last Conversations*, p. 257.
3. *Living Flame*, II:5.
4. Same as Note 2 above.
5. "That iniquity may be found unto hatred"; we adopt this
   Douai version of Ps 35, 3.